Energy from Wind and Moving Water
Energy and Control

Including:
What Do We Know About Wind and Water Energy?
Movement
Movement of Air
Movement of Water
Devices Propelled by Air
Controlling the Flow of Air and Water
Sources of Energy
Summative Task

An Integrated Unit for Grade 2
Written by:
Moore, Jackson, Johnston, Kjeldgaard, Lynch, Tonner, Tudhope,
Length of Unit: approximately: 17.5 hours

September 2001

Energy from Wind and Moving Water
Energy and Control An Integrated Unit for Grade 2

Acknowledgements
The developers are appreciative of the suggestions and comments from colleagues involved through the internal and external review process.

Participating Lead Public School Boards:
Mathematics, Grades 1-8
Grand Erie District School Board
Kawartha Pine Ridge District School Board
Renfrew District School Board

Science and Technology, Grades 1-8
Lakehead District School Board
Thames Valley District School Board
York Region District School Board

Social Studies, History and Geography, Grade 1-8
Renfrew District School Board
Thames Valley District School Board
York Region District School Board

The following organizations have supported the elementary curriculum unit project through team building and leadership:

The Council of Ontario Directors of Education
The Ontario Curriculum Centre
The Ministry of Education, Curriculum and Assessment Policy Branch

An Integrated Unit for Grade 2
Written by:

Moore, Jackson, Johnston, Kjeldgaard, Lynch, Tonner, Tudhope, Turnball

(519) 452-2000
Thames Valley District School Board

Based on a unit by:
Moore, Jackson, Johnston, Kjeldgaard, Lynch, Tonner, Tudhope, Turnball

DON - LMX
Unit Overview
Page 1

Energy from Wind and Moving Water
Energy and Control An Integrated Unit for Grade 2

Task Context
You and your friends are going on a camping trip to an island which has a steady, strong on-shore breeze. You must design and build a device to transport your group and your camping gear safely across to the island without getting either wet. Before leaving home, you need to create a model so that you can test the effectiveness of your device.

Task Summary
In this unit, students will investigate air and water as two sources of energy. They will determine that wind and moving water are renewable resources which have advantages and disadvantages in their use. Through the design and construction of wind- and water-propelled devices, students will identify factors that affect the motion and control of such devices.

Culminating Task Assessment
Students will design and build a device to transport a load across water. The device must be powered by water or air. After testing the device and making the necessary modifications, students will demonstrate the effectiveness of their device and explain how the device was constructed.

Links to Prior Knowledge
Students will be familiar with:
- the concept of living and non-living things (refer to Grade One Life Systems strand)
- the concept of the five senses (refer to Grade One Life Systems strand)
- the use of a tally and a graph to display data and the interpretation of this data (refer to Grade One Data Management strand in Mathematics)

Include prior knowledge skills and information on bulletin boards, wall charts and chart paper around the classroom. When appropriate, add to the information as the concepts are developed in the unit. For example, a vocabulary or fact bulletin board can begin with definitions or facts from related units and extended as new terms and facts are introduced.

Students could demonstrate their prior knowledge in their science and technology journals using specific concepts prompts.

Considerations

Notes to Teacher
UNIT PLANNING CONSIDERATIONS

1. Curriculum
This unit has been designed to cover the expectations in the ENERGY AND CONTROL strand in the Ontario Curriculum, Science and Technology document.

2. Integration
Each activity is designed to build skills and concepts which will be demonstrated in the summative task. Although these lessons may be taught independently, integrated learning opportunities in other subject areas may be addressed simultaneously.

Science is a form of knowledge that seeks to describe and explain the natural and physical world and its place in our universe. Technology is both a form of knowledge that uses concepts and skills from other disciplines (including science) and the application of this knowledge to meet an individual need or specific problem. Inherent in these studies is the need to both research and communicate ideas and findings, whether through specific use of scientific and technical vocabulary, or through the use of diagrams or illustrations. The study of science and technology is an opportunity for students to reinforce and extend expectations in other subject areas. When planning, teachers may wish to take advantage of opportunities to address and assess expectations from other curricula.

3. Timeframe
As science is a hands-on, resource-dependent core subject, timetabling in all grades must address the necessity of block timetabling of up to 60 minutes to thoroughly complete the lessons in this unit. Although some lessons may be covered in a shorter period of time, many of the activities and follow-ups would benefit from a longer block of time. Teachers should also be prepared to timetable at least a month to complete the unit.

4. Assessment Overview
In this unit, a variety of assessment strategies and recording devices have been included (see **BLM 2.UW.1**). The assessments provide the teacher with information on the development of students' skills in all areas of the achievement scale as outlined on page 13 in the Ontario Curriculum, Science and Technology document.

Assessment Accommodation Strategies
- consult the Individual Education Plan and adapt the assessment format (e.g., oral, practical demonstration, interview, construction, tape-recorded test) to suit the needs of the student;
- allow the student to write the main points and expand verbally; allow additional time, when required for completion;
- read or clarify questions for the student and encourage the student to rephrase questions, in his/her own words;
- provide highlighting of key words or instructions for emphasis;
- use several assessments to establish ability

5. Science and Technology Journals
Strategies, Accommodations and Adaptations
Science and technology journals give students the opportunity to construct their own understanding; to put into their own words what they are learning. They can link the observations that they make with the knowledge that they bring with them. Verbalizing ideas, both orally and in writing, is an important step in internalizing new information. Explaining and describing experiences helps learners to make connections between concepts and ideas. It also allows the teacher to track and assess the students' understanding and it provides an opportunity to correct any misunderstandings that the student may have.

In this unit, several blackline masters are provided to simplify the use of journal writing. **BLM 2.UW.5** is a cover page for the booklet. The criteria for writing a journal entry (**BLM 2.UW.6**) can be glued onto the inside cover of the journal for easy reference by students. A journal page (**BLM 2.UW.7**) has been provided if notebooks are not available. On **BLM 2.UW.8**, the title page for the Energy and Control strand is included so that each strand can be separated. It is recommended that blackline masters which are completed during the unit be included as entries into the science journal.

In order for students to be successful communicators in science and technology, the following methodology has been introduced in this unit.
a) Class Journal - During initial lessons, the teacher engages the whole class in the writing process. In order to provide opportunities for children to use rich oral language to describe, explain and respond to their shared experiences in science, the teacher acts as a scribe to record students' ideas. The class journal entries are prominently displayed as examples of "good" science writing.

b) Explaining Criteria - The teacher explains the criteria for writing a journal entry by demonstrating each statement using examples from class journal entries; for example - find all of the science and technology words used and circle these. Then, students can use the criteria to assess a piece of scientific writing. The teacher displays the writing on an overhead or chart paper and, as a class, the students discuss the piece of writing. The same procedure can be done in small groups where students find "3 Stars" (good things) and "a Wish" (things to improve next time) in a piece of writing.

c) Independent Writing - When students have had many experiences in shared writing, then they can record their ideas independently. The teacher can use the rubric on **BLM 2.UW.9** to assess the first entry and provide feedback to individual students in order to improve science writing skills. The information from this assessment could also be used for the development of class demonstrations in a specific area.

6. Inquiry and Design Models
The performance tasks in this unit use the S.P.I.C.E. Model as a method of design (see **BLM 2.UW.4**), or the I.N.S.I.T.E. Model of inquiry (see **BLM 2.UW.3**). Teachers should ensure that students are familiar with these models as a framework for approaching design or inquiry challenges.

7. Safety
Safety is an important aspect of any science and technology program. For more information on safety considerations, please see pages 8 and 9 of the Ontario Curriculum, Science and Technology document.

8. Use of Blackline Masters
Included in this unit is a large number of black-line masters. Due to the sophisticated scientific material covered in the unit and in order to meet the needs of teachers with various backgrounds, it was decided to include a broad range of black-line masters. Instead of photocopying all black-line masters the following strategies could be used:
Have students recreate the BLM as a science journal activity or in a group assignment.
Recreate BLM on a bulletin board (e.g., vocabulary/definition and fact bulletin board).
Recreate BLM as a wallchart or on chart paper.
Copy BLM on acetate and use it on an overhead projector.

9. Classroom Accommodations
All accommodations must take into account the student's Individual Education Plan. All of the tasks and activities are designed to accommodate the needs of students at different levels of abilities. Many of the activities include pictures and/or examples of a step-by-step process. These may be used at the discretion of the teacher for some or all students. As well, teachers can easily adapt the activities to allow for open-ended, student-directed tasks.
Teachers are encouraged to:
- involve the student in setting goals for work completion;
- encourage risk taking;
- provide varied opportunities for peer and/or group interactions (e.g., cooperative learning, sharing);
- teach visual strategies for journal writing and/or note making (e.g., use of diagram/picture to represent content);
- provide advance organizers to structure content (e.g., outlines, subtitles, paragraph frames);
- encourage the use of lists, advance organizers, personal planner for personal organization;
- allow opportunities for alternatives to writing (e.g., graphic representations, drama, media presentations, timelines, collages).

Energy from Wind and Moving Water
Energy and Control An Integrated Unit for Grade 2

List of Subtasks
Subtask List Page 1

1	**What Do We Know About Wind and Water Energy?**
	Students will demonstrate their prior knowledge of the topic "Energy from Wind and Water" after observing an air powered device. They will be introduced to the S.P.I.C.E. model of design.

2	**Movement**
	Students will engage in two investigations to demonstrate that movement is an outcome of energy input and that the movement of air and water produces energy.

3	**Movement of Air**
	Students will recognize that the movement of air produces energy. They will identify devices that use moving air as an energy source and will describe what problems may occur when air is still.

4	**Movement of Water**
	In this subtask, students will discover that moving water produces energy. They will use this knowledge to explain the operation of a waterwheel. Students will create and investigate their own waterwheels and water paddles.

5	**Devices Propelled by Air**
	Students will design and construct devices propelled by air and will explain the effect of wind direction and speed on the devices.

6	**Controlling the Flow of Air and Water**
	In this subtask, students will construct a device that is propelled by moving air and will experiment with their device to control the flow of air. Students will also investigate the flow of moving water by creating and controlling a fountain. Teacher demonstrations will present examples of both types of devices used in daily life.

7	**Sources of Energy**
	Students will recognize that moving air and moving water are sources of energy that are renewable and that they can be used to create electrical power. They will also determine the advantages and disadvantages of using wind and moving water as sources of energy.

8	**Summative Task**
	Students will design and build a device to transport a load across water. The device must be powered by water or air. After testing the device and making the necessary modifications, students will demonstrate the effectiveness of their device and explain how the device was constructed.

What Do We Know About Wind and Water Energy?

Energy from Wind and Moving Water
Energy and Control An Integrated Unit for Grade 2

Subtask 1
120 mins

Description
Students will demonstrate their prior knowledge of the topic "Energy from Wind and Water" after observing an air powered device. They will be introduced to the S.P.I.C.E. model of design.

Expectations
2s49	• demonstrate an understanding of the movement of air and of water as sources of energy;
2s50	• design and construct devices that are propelled by moving air or moving water;
2s51	• identify wind and moving water as renewable sources of energy and determine the advantages and disadvantages of using them.

Groupings
Students Working As A Whole Class
Students Working Individually

Teaching / Learning Strategies
Demonstration
Discussion
Direct Teaching

Assessment

Assessment Strategies
Questions And Answers (oral)
Select Response

Assessment Recording Devices
Anecdotal Record

Teaching / Learning

1. Prior to presenting the lesson, a "hovercraft" should be created by the teacher. Directions for the "hovercraft" are found on **BLM 2.1.2**.

2. Introduce this unit by explaining to the students that the class will be learning about energy from wind and water.

3. Continue the discussion by asking the students: "What is energy?" If they are unable to come up with a definition, explain that "energy" is the ability to do work or make things move or change.

4. Show the class the "hovercraft." Have the children predict what they think will happen when the clothes pin is removed. Ask the students if they think the same thing will happen if the hovercraft is in water. Demonstrate how the vehicle operates on a flat surface and then in water. (The hovercraft should skim across the surface as the air flows out of the balloon.)

5. Ask the students what energy has to do with the "hovercraft." Also ask them how moving air (wind) and moving water help to produce energy. Have the students keep their responses to themselves.

6. In a large group, discuss student responses. Create a chart for each question where additional information can be recorded or ideas can be changed throughout the unit.

7. To assess prior knowledge of the concepts in this unit, have the students complete **BLM 2.1.3a - Part 1: Assessing Prior Knowledge**. This sheet should be dated and filed for use at the end of the unit.

8. In order to create student interest in the unit, provide a brief description of the culminating task.

9. Produce a chart of the S.P.I.C.E. Model of Design (**BLM 2.UW.4**) and post it in the classroom. Using the

What Do We Know About Wind and Water Energy?

Energy from Wind and Moving Water
Energy and Control An Integrated Unit for Grade 2

Subtask 1
120 mins

chart, review the S.P.I.C.E. model with the students. Explain that they will use the model later in the unit to help them design and construct a transportation device. Present the letters for the S.P.I.C.E. model down the length of a piece of chart paper. Throughout the unit, students will construct various devices which use wind and water energy. List these devices on the chart paper beside "S," as possible solutions to the "summative task problem."

10. To reinforce the understanding of the S.P.I.C.E. model, have students view the story "Between the Walls" from the video "Look Again 1." In various places, stop the video to discuss the "situation" (mouse has entered the young girl's house), the "problem" (how is the young girl going to catch the mouse without harming it), the "searching for ideas" (tries a real mouse-trap and observes what it would do to the mouse), the "constructing" (builds and tests various traps) and the "evaluating" (traps the mouse and allows it to escape unharmed). To add interest, you may wish to stop the video as the problem has been identified. Students could draw and label their solutions to the problem before viewing the solutions the young girl tries. Also students could describe the advantages and disadvantages of the materials being used to build each trap. Suggestions could be made to improve each trap as it is shown in the video.

11. Distribute the "Letter to Parents" (**BLM 2.1.1**) to provide parents/guardians with information about this unit of study, and to request their help in providing materials students will require to construct their transportation devices.

12. Use the anecdotal record sheet on **BLM 2.UW.2a** to track student understanding of basic concepts. Possible teacher comments are presented on **BLM 2.UW.2b**.

13. Have students complete **BLM 2.1.3b - Part 2: Assessing Knowledge** at the end of the unit.

Adaptations

All accommodations must take into account the student's Individual Education Plan. All of the tasks and activities are designed to accommodate the needs of students at different levels of abilities. For detailed strategies see number 9 in the Notes to Teacher section of the Unit Overview.

Resources

- **BLM 2.1.1** BLM_1.1.cwk
- **BLM 2.1.2** BLM_1.2.cwk
- **BLM 2.1.3a** BLM_1.3a.cwk
- **BLM 2.1.3b** BLM_1.3b.cwk
- **Look Again 1 - Sense of Sound** National Film Board of Canada - Program Sales
  150 John Street Toronto, Ontario M5V 3C3
- one balloon
- stiff cardboard or plastic margarine lid
- clothespin
- liquid soap

What Do We Know About Wind and Water Energy?

Energy from Wind and Moving Water

Energy and Control An Integrated Unit for Grade 2

Subtask 1

120 mins

- cork with a hole through the middle
- chart paper

Notes to Teacher

1. Assessment of Student Progress
At the end of the unit, teachers can use the information students recorded on **BLM 2.1.3a** and **BLM 2.1.3b** to help assess student progress.

2. Video - Look Again 1 (10 min. 18 sec.)
"Between the Walls" is the story of a young girl who discovers a mouse that lives between the walls of her home. When the mouse is threatened, she is presented with a problem; because she wants to save the mouse. Teachers can provide students with an opportunity to predict how the girl deals with her dilemma, before letting them see the realistic and sensitive solution at which she eventually arrives.

Teacher Reflections

Energy from Wind and Moving Water
Energy and Control An Integrated Unit for Grade 2

Movement
Subtask 2
60 mins

Description
Students will engage in two investigations to demonstrate that movement is an outcome of energy input and that the movement of air and water produces energy.

Expectations
2s52   – identify movement as an outcome of energy input (e.g., fuel enables cars, trucks, and buses to move; electricity enables the fan in the kitchen to move; food enables humans to move);

2s53   – recognize that it is the movement of air and water that produces energy and that air and water are not by themselves sources of energy;

Groupings
Students Working In Small Groups
Students Working Individually
Students Working As A Whole Class

Teaching / Learning Strategies
Inquiry
Discussion
Learning Log/ Journal

Assessment

Assessment Strategies
Learning Log

Assessment Recording Devices
Rubric

Teaching / Learning

1. Display a variety of devices which move as a result of energy input (e.g. fan, clock, spring toy, egg beaters). Have the students name the source of energy and the resulting action (energy input/output). Remind students that energy is the ability to do work and it can make things move or change.

2. Have students explore the classroom as well as the playground to compile a class chart of things that move. Using this information, compile a chart with the following headings: DEVICE, ENERGY SOURCE, ACTIVITY. Reinforce the concept that energy is the ability to do work.

3. Distribute **BLM 2.2.1** and **BLM 2.2.2**. Review the challenge question and the other information found on each task card. Allow students to work in pairs to complete each task.

4. When students have completed both challenge tasks, as a class, review the results by discussing the "Think About" questions. Elicit the following information: Wind (moving air) and moving water are sources of energy. It is the *movement* of air and water that produces the energy to move the cup and boat, respectively.

Explain that moving air and water are considered "renewable" sources of energy. Ask students why moving air and moving water are called renewable sources of energy (because there is always more air and water that can be used as an energy source).

5. In their science and technology journals, have students briefly outline each challenge and tell what they learned. To help students with their journal entries post and briefly discuss the following questions:
a) How did you make the cup move without touching it? (Answers will vary.)
b) How did you make the toy boat/ping pong ball move across the water without touching it? (Answers will vary.)
c) Why are wind and water sources of energy? (Because they can make things move or change.)
d) What are the advantages of using wind and water energy? (They are renewable sources of energy.

Energy from Wind and Moving Water
Energy and Control An Integrated Unit for Grade 2

Movement
Subtask 2
60 mins

They can be used again and again.)

6. Read and discuss print resources such as: *Energy Forever? Water Power* pages 4 and 5 as well as *Energy Forever? Wind Power* pages 4 and 5. In these books, air and water are introduced as sources of energy and some advantages and disadvantages of each are mentioned.

7. Teachers can assess students' knowledge of basic concepts, communication skills and relating to the world using the rubric on **BLM 2.UW.9**.

Adaptations
All accommodations must take into account the student's Individual Education Plan. All of the tasks and activities are designed to accommodate the needs of students at different levels of abilities. For detailed strategies see number 9 in the Notes to Teacher section of the Unit Overview.

Resources

BLM 2.2.1	BLM_2.1.cwk
BLM 2.2.2	BLM_2.2.cwk
Energy Forever? Water Power	Ian Graham
Energy Forever? Wind Power	Ian Graham
plastic cups	
empty juice boxes	
toy boats or ping pong balls	
long container of water (wallpaper tray)	
variety of devices (fan, clock, spring toy, beater)	

Notes to Teacher

The purpose of challenge #1 is to create wind (moving air) by continually squeezing and releasing the juice box and directing the flow of air to move the cup. The purpose of challenge #2 is to show how moving water can make objects move. If children blow on the cup or boat, ask them how else they might cause the objects to move.

Teacher Reflections

Energy from Wind and Moving Water
Energy and Control An Integrated Unit for Grade 2

Movement of Air
Subtask 3
60 mins

Description
Students will recognize that the movement of air produces energy. They will identify devices that use moving air as an energy source and will describe what problems may occur when air is still.

Expectations

2s49	• demonstrate an understanding of the movement of air and of water as sources of energy;
2s50	• design and construct devices that are propelled by moving air or moving water;
2s53	– recognize that it is the movement of air and water that produces energy and that air and water are not by themselves sources of energy;
2s57	– ask questions about and identify needs and problems related to the use of wind and moving water as energy sources, and explore possible answers and solutions (e.g., describe how moving water is used to produce electricity; describe how windmills were used to grind grain into flour);
2s62	– identify devices that use moving air and moving water as energy sources (e.g., windmills, water wheels), and describe what happens to these devices when the air or water is still;
2s63	– list activities that are affected by moving water and wind (e.g., fishing, sailing, flying a plane);

Groupings
Students Working As A Whole Class
Students Working Individually

Teaching / Learning Strategies
Discussion
Model Making
Oral Explanation
Learning Log/ Journal

Assessment

Assessment Strategies
Exhibition/demonstration
Questions And Answers (oral)
Response Journal

Assessment Recording Devices
Checklist

Teaching / Learning

1. Begin the lesson by asking the question: "What is wind?" Using the suggestions from the students explain that wind is moving air, a renewable energy source. Moving air creates air power. Have students think of objects that moving air (wind) moves. Create a chart of suggestions (e.g., sailboat, flag, hotair balloon).

2. In order to demonstrate the wind cycle, create shapes to represent the sun, the land, cool air and water (refer to **BLM 2.3.1 - Teacher Reference - The Wind Cycle**). Have students assist in creating the wind cycle on the board by placing the land and sun shapes on the board and explaining that the air over the land is heated by the sun and rises. Continue building the wind cycle.

3. Provide students with a copy of **BLM 2.3.2** and label the diagram together. Have students complete the cloze activity which describes the movement of air and the creation of wind.

4. Have students construct a wind wiggler to demonstrate the movement of objects by air. Students colour the three types of wind wigglers on **BLM 2.3.3, BLM 2.3.4** and **BLM 2.3.5** and cut out the wigglers along the solid lines. Then a piece of string is taped to the centre of each shape.

5. Before testing the wind wigglers, have students predict which wiggler will work the best. Allow time for students to record their predictions in their science and technology journals. Have them give a reason for their choice.

6. Distribute **BLM 2.3.6 - Testing Wind Wigglers Chart**, review it with students, then have them conduct a test to evaluate how well the wind wigglers work. Students can test the wigglers by taking them outside on a breezy day, by hanging them over a radiator or by using a variable speed fan. After the testing is complete,

Energy from Wind and Moving Water
Energy and Control An Integrated Unit for Grade 2

Movement of Air
Subtask 3
60 mins

discuss the questions on the bottom of **BLM 2.3.6**.

7. In a follow-up discussion, have students suggest activities which are affected by wind (i.e., flag flying, drying clothes on a clothesline, sailing, sailboarding, hot air ballooning, gliding, throwing things such as a baseball, boomerang, frisbee, parachuting, kite-flying, flying a plane or dispersing seeds).

8. Use **BLM 2.3.7 - Checklist for Wind Wiggler Activity** to evaluate the students' design and inquiry skills and to assess their understanding of the concepts investigated in this subtask.

Adaptations
All accommodations must take into account the student's Individual Education Plan. All of the tasks and activities are designed to accommodate the needs of students at different levels of abilities. For detailed strategies see number 9 in the Notes to Teacher section of the Unit Overview.

Resources

BLM 2.3.1	BLM_3.1.cwk
BLM 2.3.2	BLM_3.2.pdf
BLM 2.3.3	BLM_3.3.cwk
BLM 2.3.4	BLM_3.4.cwk
BLM 2.3.5	BLM_3.5.cwk
BLM 2.3.6	BLM_3.6.cwk
BLM 2.3.7	BLM_3.7.cwk
Energy Forever? Wind Power	Ian Graham
crayons	
string	
tape	
chart paper	
oscillating fan	

Energy from Wind and Moving Water
Energy and Control An Integrated Unit for Grade 2

Movement of Air
Subtask 3
60 mins

Notes to Teacher
The Wind Cycle - the sun warms the atmosphere more in some areas than in others and the result is uneven heating of the air. Temperature differences occur and, therefore, warm air rises. Nature tries to equalize and cool air moves in to replace the warm air.

In the experiment with the wind wigglers, students are testing the various shapes to see which shape moves best in the wind. The circular shape moves best because it is more streamlined.

Teacher Reflections

Energy from Wind and Moving Water
Energy and Control An Integrated Unit for Grade 2

Movement of Water
Subtask 4
180 mins

Description
In this subtask, students will discover that moving water produces energy. They will use this knowledge to explain the operation of a waterwheel. Students will create and investigate their own waterwheels and water paddles.

Expectations

2s49	• demonstrate an understanding of the movement of air and of water as sources of energy;
2s50	• design and construct devices that are propelled by moving air or moving water;
2s53	– recognize that it is the movement of air and water that produces energy and that air and water are not by themselves sources of energy;
2s57	– ask questions about and identify needs and problems related to the use of wind and moving water as energy sources, and explore possible answers and solutions (e.g., describe how moving water is used to produce electricity; describe how windmills were used to grind grain into flour);
2s60	– record relevant observations, findings, and measurements, using written language, pictures, and charts (e.g., draw a diagram of their device; prepare a chart to present data on the distance travelled by their device over time);
2s62	– identify devices that use moving air and moving water as energy sources (e.g., windmills, water wheels), and describe what happens to these devices when the air or water is still;
2s63	– list activities that are affected by moving water and wind (e.g., fishing, sailing, flying a plane);

Groupings
Students Working As A Whole Class
Students Working Individually
Students Working In Pairs

Teaching / Learning Strategies
Discussion
Demonstration
Model Making
Learning Log/ Journal

Assessment

Assessment Strategies
Observation
Exhibition/demonstration
Response Journal

Assessment Recording Devices
Checklist
Rubric

Teaching / Learning
Part A: The Water Wheel

1. Introduce this subtask by showing pictures of examples of still water (lake) and of moving water (Niagara Falls). Explain that both pictures are similar because they contain water. Ask students to explain what is different about the water in the pictures. Pose the question: "Where else have you seen moving water?" (waves in ocean, swiftly flowing rivers or streams, waterfalls, rapids, water coming from a tap). Review that moving water can be a source of energy.

2. Hold up a jug of coloured water. Present the following problem: "Can you think of a way to get the water in this jug to do work for me?" Have students brainstorm ideas. If there are no suggestions, explain that the water in the jug is not moving and it is waiting to be given energy (has potential energy). Ask: "What could I do to make the water move?" (Tip the jug so the water begins to pour out) Ask: "Have you ever seen a device which uses moving water to work?" (Water wheel.)

3. Constructing a Water Wheel:
Distribute **BLM 2.4.1 - Water Wheel Patterns**. Provide each student with a plastic lid.
Instructions:
- cut the edge off the plastic lid
- cut out the circle and tape it to the lid
- cut along the dotted lines towards the centre of the lid as illustrated on BLM 2.4.1

Energy from Wind and Moving Water
Energy and Control An Integrated Unit for Grade 2

Movement of Water
Subtask 4
180 mins

- remove the paper circle from the lid
- fold each section of the lid in half to form the blades of the water wheel (each blade forms a cup to catch the water).

At this point the students will need assistance:
- help them poke a hole in the centre of the lid
- wiggle a pencil in the hole to make it larger, then insert a straw into the hole
- put a wooden skewer through the straw
- to operate the wheel, hold the ends of the skewer and place the wheel under a stream of moving water.

Note that the pattern may need to be adjusted for the size of the lids students are using.

4. Testing the Water Wheel:
Distribute copies of **BLM 2.4.2** to students.
a) To test the movement of the wheel, select either method A or B below:
Method A - divide the students into teams of four. Explain the roles of team members. One member pours the jug of water, one member holds the ends of the water wheel, one member observes and counts the rotations of the wheel and the other member fills the water jug.
Method B - students work in partners. One person holds the water wheel under a faucet and counts the rotations while the other partner controls the water flow rate and watches the clock for thirty seconds.

Observations about what happens to the wheel when the water is still, moving slowly and moving quickly are recorded on **BLM 2.4.2**.

b) To demonstrate that the water wheel can do work, have students tape the axle (straw) to the water wheel. Attach a thread to the straw and tie a light object at the other end of the thread. Holding the ends of the skewer, the students place the water wheel under a stream of water and record their observations on **BLM 2.4.2** (as the wheel turns, the axle turns, drawing the object upward).

5. Follow-up:
Have students discuss their observations. Review the concept that moving water is the source of energy which turns the water wheel. When the water wheel turns, it does work for people. Ask the question: "What could you do to change your water wheel to make it more efficient ?" Have students think about an idea, share their idea with a partner and then share their idea with the class.

6. Continue the discussion by making a chart of activities which are affected by moving water (i.e., boating, swimming, surfing, sailboarding, fishing, jet-skiing).

7. To assess understanding of basic knowledge and the students' design and inquiry skills, use the checklist on **BLM 2.4.3**.

Part B: Making Paddles

1. Using a book such as *Energy Forever? Water Power*, explain how the water wheel was invented (pages 16 and 17) and how the various types of water wheels operate (i.e., overshot, undershot and horizontal, pages 22 and 23). Have students suggest which type of water wheel would be the most effective and why. Discuss how the water wheel was used to grind grain into flour.

2. Working in partners, have the students create a water paddle following the directions on **BLM 2.4.4**. (See construction steps on **BLM 2.4.5**.) Depending upon the reading level of the students, you may wish to read the instructions as the students construct the water paddle.

3. Ask students what happens when water is poured onto the blades of the paddle. Have students predict what would happen if water was poured onto the paddle from different heights. In teams of four, students

Energy from Wind and Moving Water
Energy and Control An Integrated Unit for Grade 2

Movement of Water
Subtask 4
180 mins

test their paddles to observe what happens at various heights.   Observations are recorded on **BLM 2.4.6**.

4. These water paddles must be kept to use again in Subtask #5.

5. Discuss possible uses of a water paddle (create propulsion for boats).

6. In their science and technology journals, students explain what they learned about water paddles and explain how water paddles are used for propulsion or to do work.

7. Use the journal writing rubric on **BLM 2.UW.9** to assess the students' understanding of basic concepts in this lesson.

Adaptations
All accommodations must take into account the student's Individual Education Plan. All of the tasks and activities are designed to accommodate the needs of students at different levels of abilities. For detailed strategies see number 9 in the Notes to Teacher section of the Unit Overview.

Resources

BLM 2.4.1	BLM_4.1.cwk
BLM 2.4.2	BLM_4.2.cwk
BLM 2.4.3	BLM_4.3.cwk
BLM 2.4.4	BLM_4.4.cwk
BLM 2.4.5	BLM_4.5.pdf
BLM 2.4.6	BLM_4.6.cwk
Energy Forever? Water Power	Ian Graham
plastic lids	
straws	
jug of coloured water	
wooden barbecue skewers	
tape	
thread	
small objects	
chart paper	
pencils	

Energy from Wind and Moving Water
Energy and Control An Integrated Unit for Grade 2

Movement of Water
Subtask 4
180 mins

- plastic film canisters
- 2 L ice cream containers
- duct tape
- pictures of still water and Niagara Falls
- cups for pouring water
- awl for punching holes

Notes to Teacher

Safety
Teachers should remind students to cut the end off the skewers to ensure the safety of the students.

Water Wheels - History
The water wheel is one of the oldest known sources of power. The first reference to its use dates back to about 4000 B.C., where, in a poem by an early Greek writer, Antipater, it tells about the freedom from the toil of young women who operated small handmills to grind corn. Water wheels were later used to drive sawmills, pumps, forge bellows, tilt-hammers, trip hammers and to power textile mills. Prior to the development of steam power during the Industrial Revolution, water wheels were the only sources of power. Thus, most towns existed near a river on which water wheels could be used.

Water Wheels - Movement
The movement of the waterwheel may vary depending on the angle in which the water hits the blades or the angle in which the wheel is being held.

Teacher Reflections

Energy from Wind and Moving Water
Energy and Control An Integrated Unit for Grade 2

Devices Propelled by Air
Subtask 5
90 mins

Description
Students will design and construct devices propelled by air and will explain the effect of wind direction and speed on the devices.

Expectations

2s55	– design and construct a device propelled by air (e.g., a kite, a pinwheel, a balloon rocket);
2s61	– communicate the procedures and results of investigations and explorations for specific purposes, using drawings, demonstrations, and oral and written descriptions (e.g., prepare a showcase of different devices that are propelled by wind energy; explain the effect of wind direction and speed on the displacement of wind-propelled devices).
2s49	• demonstrate an understanding of the movement of air and of water as sources of energy;
2s50	• design and construct devices that are propelled by moving air or moving water;
2s51	• identify wind and moving water as renewable sources of energy and determine the advantages and disadvantages of using them.

Groupings
Students Working As A Whole Class
Students Working In Small Groups
Students Working Individually

Teaching / Learning Strategies
Brainstorming
Discussion
Model Making
Oral Explanation
Learning Log/ Journal

Assessment

Assessment Strategies
Questions And Answers (oral)
Learning Log
Observation

Assessment Recording Devices
Rubric

Teaching / Learning
Part A: Sails

1. Pose the question: "How do we use the wind?" In their science and technology journals, students independently compile a list of ways that we use the wind. Students then pair and share with a partner to add ideas to their lists. The final lists are shared with the class. The teacher records a master list on the chalkboard or chart paper while the presentations are made.

2. Explain to the students that they will make their own sails out of materials available in the classroom (tissue paper, construction paper, fabric). The sails are tested on a string track to see which travels the longest distance. Attach a string to a fan and to a chair across the room. Encourage students to think about which material they will use and why. Students choose which material(s) to use and in their science and technology journals, draw a design of their sails. Students then create sails according to their designs.

3. Connect students' sails to the track with paper clips at the end closer to the fan. Turn on the fan and measure how far each sail goes. Record the distances on a class chart.

4. In their science and technology journals, students will record the distance that their sails travelled and compare their results to those of their classmates. Students should suggest possible reasons for the differences. Answers will vary and can be assessed with the Journal Assessment Rubric (**BLM 2.UW.5**).

5. As a class, discuss the possible advantages and disadvantages of each sail material and determine which sail used the energy from wind most effectively.

Energy from Wind and Moving Water
Energy and Control An Integrated Unit for Grade 2

Devices Propelled by Air
Subtask 5
90 mins

6. In a large group, discuss how we use the wind's energy to do work. Explain that in ancient times, people used the wind as a natural energy source to propel sail boats and turn the sails of windmills. Explain that all moving things have energy. Moving energy is called "kinetic energy". This energy can be used to grind grain, pump water, saw logs, make electricity or move boats.

Part B - Making a Pinwheel

1. Students construct a pinwheel to investigate a device which is propelled by air (wind). Point out that pinwheels are similar to windmills, because they both rely on wind energy which is converted to kinetic energy (energy of motion). Ensure that safety using tools is addressed prior to starting the activity. Remind students not to extend nails beyond the wood (see BLM 2.5.1 # 8).

2. Provide each student with **BLM 2.5.1 - The Pinwheel** and **BLM 2.5.2 - How to Make a Pinwheel Instructions**. Allow time for students to read the instructions and to study the illustrations. Depending upon the reading level of the students, the teacher may wish to read the instructions as the students construct the pinwheel. Before the students construct their pinwheels, review the procedures and answer any questions which arise. Note: This activity is an opportunity for students to develop skill in reading non-fiction material and in following pictorial instructions.

3. Encourage students to experiment with their pinwheels to discover the answers to the questions on **BLM 2.5.3a, Part 1**, then have them complete **Part 2**. (**Part 2** asks them to evaluate their pinwheel and consider modifications.)

4. Using **BLM 2.5.3b** as a guide, discuss student responses to **Parts 1 and 2**.

5. Follow-up: This is a good opportunity to identify wind as a renewable resource and to discuss the advantages and disadvantages of wind as a source of energy.
- Tell students that wind is a renewable resource because there is always more air (wind) available to use as a source of power. This is an advantage because it is readily available (lots of it) and it is free.
- The windmill is an example of how we use the wind to help us do work. Like the pinwheel, the windmill converts wind energy to kinetic energy (energy of movement). We use the kinetic energy of the windmill to do work (grind grains, etc.). In other words, we harness the wind's power to help us do work.
- Ask the students what would happen to the windmill if the speed or direction of the wind changed. (It might not work as effectively.) "What would happen if the wind didn't blow?" (The windmill wouldn't function so no work would be done.) Point out that these are disadvantages.

Adaptations
All accommodations must take into account the student's Individual Education Plan. All of the tasks and activities are designed to accommodate the needs of students at different levels of abilities. For detailed strategies see number 9 in the Notes to Teacher section of the Unit Overview.

Resources

	BLM 2.5.1	BLM_5.1.cwk
	BLM 2.5.2	BLM_5.2.cwk

Energy from Wind and Moving Water
Energy and Control An Integrated Unit for Grade 2

Devices Propelled by Air
Subtask 5
90 mins

📄	**BLM 2.5.3a**	BLM_5.3a.cwk
📄	**BLM 2.5.3b**	BLM_5.3b.cwk
📚	**Energy Forever? Wind Power**	Ian Graham
	thread	
	paper clips	
	construction paper	
	various kinds of fabric	
	tissue paper	
	Jinks wood	
	one inch nails	
	water in jugs	
	crayons for colouring the pinwheel	
	stopwatches	
	water paddles from Subtask 4	

Notes to Teacher

Teacher Reflections

Controlling the Flow of Air and Water

Energy from Wind and Moving Water
Energy and Control An Integrated Unit for Grade 2

Subtask 6
180 mins

Description
In this subtask, students will construct a device that is propelled by moving air and will experiment with their device to control the flow of air. Students will also investigate the flow of moving water by creating and controlling a fountain. Teacher demonstrations will present examples of both types of devices used in daily life.

Expectations

2s50	• design and construct devices that are propelled by moving air or moving water;
2s56	– design and construct a system that controls the flow of water and/or air using a variety of mechanisms (e.g., a musical instrument, a fountain, valves, a dam);
2s57	– ask questions about and identify needs and problems related to the use of wind and moving water as energy sources, and explore possible answers and solutions (e.g., describe how moving water is used to produce electricity; describe how windmills were used to grind grain into flour);
2s65	– describe how gravity and the shape of different structures affect the behaviour and use of moving water (e.g., water in waterfalls, taps, fountains).

Groupings
Students Working As A Whole Class
Students Working Individually
Students Working In Small Groups

Teaching / Learning Strategies
Demonstration
Experimenting
Discussion
Learning Log/ Journal
Problem Posing

Assessment

Assessment Strategies
Learning Log
Observation

Assessment Recording Devices
Rubric

Teaching / Learning
Part A: Balloon Jets - Controlling the Flow of Air

Safety Note: Some students may be allergic to latex in the balloons. If a student has such an allergy, ensure non-latex ballons are available. Repeated handling of balloons may produce a reaction to latex.

1. To begin a discussion about controlling the flow of air, inflate a balloon and let it go. Ask students to describe what happened to the balloon and why it happened. (The balloon is propelled around the room in various directions. Air which is escaping from the small opening in the balloon makes the balloon move. The balloon moves in the opposite direction to the direction of the escaping air.)

2. Ask students: "What provided the energy for the balloon to move?" (The air in the balloon provided the energy for the balloon to move. The more air placed in the balloon, the greater the potential energy. If the energy is released through a small opening, it creates a propulsive force and moves the balloon. The air was supplied by the teacher who transferred some of his/her energy to the balloon by inflating it.)

3. Have students suggest ways in which the movement of air from the balloon can be controlled so that we can get the balloon to go in one direction only. Demonstrate one method of controlling the direction of the escaping air by inserting a straw into the neck of the balloon and securing the opening with duct tape. (Removing the ring of rubber at the neck of the balloon allows you to create a better seal.) Test the "balloon jet" to see in which direction it moves.

4. Demonstrate how to make a "land rover" using a balloon jet for propulsion. Cut a drinking box in half

Energy from Wind and Moving Water
Energy and Control An Integrated Unit for Grade 2

Controlling the Flow of Air and Water
Subtask 6
180 mins

lengthwise. Make a hole in the back part of the box. Lay the balloon jet on top of the drinking box and poke the straw through the hole. Inflate the balloon jet using the straw. Allow the "land rover" to travel along a desk and note the direction of the moving air and the direction in which the rover moves. Show students how to add a clothespin to the straw to act as an on-off valve.

5. Model the I.N.S.I.T.E. process (see Notes to Teachers section in the Unit Overview). Ask the question: "What could you do to control the flow of air from your balloon jet? How could you prove this?" Have the students brainstorm ideas to solve this problem.

6. Divide students into teams of three to conduct an experiment about controlling the flow of air from their balloon jets. Each student needs three balloon jets with varying lengths of straws. Students inflate the balloons so they are the same size each time and then measure the distance the land rover travels. Team results are recorded on **BLM 2.6.1**.

7. When teams have completed the experiment, they share their results with the class. (The experiment should demonstrate that the longer the straw, the farther the land rover will travel. When the rate of air flow is slower, the balloon continues moving for a longer period of time. Note: Friction could be a strong variable in this experiment.)

8. Explain that the movement of air is controlled in many systems in our world. Examples of systems where the flow of air goes in certain directions to do different jobs are: heating vent systems, opening and closing windows, stove or bathroom fans, woodwind and brass musical instruments. Demonstrate the control of the flow of air with a bicycle pump or a ball pump. Have a student place his/her hand on a deflated ball. By raising the handle to various heights, show how different forces control the flow of air entering the ball.

9. If possible, show a variety of woodwind or brass instruments. Demonstrate how the instruments control the flow of air to make high and low or loud and soft sounds.

Part B: Fountains - Controlling the Flow of Water

1. Explain that humans have also learned to control water movement or flow to do different jobs. Show students a tall tin can filled with water. Ask: "What would happen if a hole was punched in the side of the container?" After punching the hole, ask students why the water flows out of the container. (Gravity, air pressure plus the weight of the water above the hole causes water to flow out of the container). Have students suggest ways to stop the water from coming out of the hole and try one of the methods. Ask: "How could I get the water to flow again?"

2. Have students suggest examples of systems where there is a flow of water that can be stopped and started again. List the suggestions on chart paper and add any of the following systems: taps, fountains, toilets, hoses, sprinklers, watering cans, eavestroughs, drains, pumps, dams, lock systems for boats, irrigation systems. Ask: "How do these systems help people?" Show pictures which illustrate a dam for hydroelectric power and water jets for mining gold.

3. Model the I.N.S.I.T.E. process (see Notes to Teacher section of the Unit Overview). Explain that the children in Warmsville are very hot during the summer months. They think that a large water fountain at the park would be a fun way to cool off. Have students suggest ways to create a "fountain" using a plastic container and an awl. (If holes are poked at different levels, one under the other, a fountain effect is created when the container is filled with water.)

4. Push three holes into a container at different levels. Have students predict what will happen when the container is filled with water. (The water from the lowest hole will shoot the furthest due to the pressure on it from the water above it.)

Energy from Wind and Moving Water
Energy and Control An Integrated Unit for Grade 2

Controlling the Flow of Air and Water
Subtask 6
180 mins

5. Divide students into teams of four. The challenge for each group is to create a "fountain" that shoots water the farthest. They may use a variety of containers. There is a limit on the number of holes which can be used and the holes may be placed anywhere on the container. (A hammer, nails, and safety goggles can be used to punch holes in tin containers. Scissors can be used for punching holes in plastic containers.) Teachers should train students in the correct use of tools such as scissors, hammers, and nails. Adult assistance (parent volunteers) may be necessary for this activity. Students must also devise a method of controlling the flow of water from their system.

6. To test the fountains, use a large basin or take the fountains outside. Measure the distance for each group in non-standard or standard units and record the results on **BLM 2.6.2**. Ensure that each group demonstrates the method they designed to stop the flow of water in their fountain. After testing the fountains, discuss why some of the fountains shot further than others. (Water is under greater pressure at the bottom of the can so if a hole was placed there, the fountain would go farther and last longer.)

7. Present the following question for group problem-solving: "How does a city get its water?" Have students use the information learned about fountains to try to explain this system. (Water is pumped into a reservoir or water tower. This water is higher than most of the buildings in the city. When a tap or faucet is opened, water flows because of gravity.)

8. Using the materials listed on the diagram on **BLM 2.6.3**, demonstrate how the water from the reservoir (water jug) would flow through the pipes (flexible tubing) into a house (margarine container). Ask the question: "If I fill the reservoir with water, what will happen?" (Water will flow continually into the margarine container.) Have students suggest a way to control the flow of water into the house. Connect a valve to the flexible tubing to control the flow of water. Continue the demonstration by asking how we can get water to go to more than one house. Again have students provide suggestions to solve this problem. (Add more flexible tubing and valves.)

9. In their science and technology journals, have students choose two systems that control the flow of water. They draw a picture of the system and explain how the flow of water is controlled. Students tell how this object helps people.

10. In order to assess students' understanding of basic concepts, communication skills and relating to the world, use the journal writing rubric on **BLM 2.UW.9**.

Adaptations
All accommodations must take into account the student's Individual Education Plan. All of the tasks and activities are designed to accommodate the needs of students at different levels of abilities. For detailed strategies see number 9 in the Notes to Teacher section of the Unit Overview.

Resources

	BLM 2.6.1	BLM_6.1.cwk
	BLM 2.6.2	BLM_6.2.cwk
	BLM 2.6.3	BLM_6.3.cwk
	Energy Forever? Water Power	Ian Graham

Controlling the Flow of Air and Water

Energy from Wind and Moving Water
Energy and Control An Integrated Unit for Grade 2

Subtask 6
180 mins

- balloons
- straws
- duct tape
- 1 litre milk cartons cut in half lengthwise
- plastic or tin containers of different shapes
- water
- masking tape
- plasticine
- large plastic basins or a sink
- scissors for punching holes
- hammer, nails and goggles for punching holes
- water jug
- rubber stopper
- flexible tubing and valves
- bicycle pump or ball pump
- woodwind or brass musical instruments
- deflated ball

Notes to Teacher

Teacher Reflections

Energy from Wind and Moving Water
Energy and Control An Integrated Unit for Grade 2

Sources of Energy
Subtask 7
60 mins

Description
Students will recognize that moving air and moving water are sources of energy that are renewable and that they can be used to create electrical power. They will also determine the advantages and disadvantages of using wind and moving water as sources of energy.

Expectations

2s49	• demonstrate an understanding of the movement of air and of water as sources of energy;
2s51	• identify wind and moving water as renewable sources of energy and determine the advantages and disadvantages of using them.
2s54	– identify various ways in which moving water is used as a form of energy (e.g., hydroelectricity, tidal energy).
2s59	– use appropriate vocabulary in describing their investigations, explorations, and observations (e.g., use terms such as renewable and movement when describing energy);
2s64	– recognize that moving air and moving water can be sources of energy for electrical power;

Groupings
Students Working As A Whole Class
Students Working In Small Groups
Students Working Individually

Teaching / Learning Strategies
Discussion
Sketching To Learn

Assessment

Assessment Strategies
Observation

Assessment Recording Devices
Anecdotal Record

Teaching / Learning
Part A: Hydroelectricity

1. As a group, view the video "Changes in Energy" (10 minutes in length). View the first part of the video. Discuss that we need electricity as the energy source for a variety of appliances. Ask: "Where does electricity come from?" Have students provide suggestions. While viewing the conclusion to the video, have students watch for the answer to the above question.

2. Discuss how moving water is transformed into electricity as shown in the above video. (Water flows from a reservoir of water over a turbine. The flow of the water makes the turbine turn creating electricity.) To illustrate this test, create a simple diagram of this for students to see.

3. Have students complete **BLM 2.7.1** by drawing a simple diagram of a hydroelectric plant and filling in the appropriate responses in the blanks provided. Responses for this are shown on **BLM 2.7.3**.

Part B: A Wind Farm

1. Pose the question: "How do you think wind is transformed into electricity?" Show the class the picture of the wind farm and ask: "What are the devices in the picture?", "What are they used for?," and "How do you think that they work?" Show the other pictures of wind turbines and generators. Explain to students that the devices are wind turbines and when there are a number of them together, they are called a "wind farm." They are placed in areas where the wind often blows. Scientists look carefully at locations to determine if there will be enough wind to make the wind turbines work. When the wind blows, the blades turn and the turbine produces electricity.

2. Create a simple diagram of a wind turbine for the students to see.

Sources of Energy
Subtask 7

Energy from Wind and Moving Water
Energy and Control An Integrated Unit for Grade 2

60 mins

3. Have students complete **BLM 2.7.2** by drawing a simple diagram of a wind turbine and filling in the appropriate responses in the blanks provided. Responses for this are shown on **BLM 2.7.3**.

Part C: Renewable Resources and Non-Renewable Resources

1. Discuss the terms "renewable resources" and "non-renewable resources" and develop a class definition for both terms. (Renewable - Natural energy that can be replaced. Non-renewable - Energy sources that are limited and that cannot be replaced once they are used up.) Once a definition has been created, post it in the classroom. Ask students to suggest resources which they think are renewable.

2. If students do not suggest that wind and water are renewable resources, explain that both of these resources are renewable. Explain that there are advantages and disadvantages to these renewable resources.

3. Have students work in groups of three or four. Ask each group to write down the advantages and disadvantages of each of these resources. Each group should appoint a spokesperson and groups should take turns sharing their ideas. These responses should be recorded on chart paper.

4. If the groups do not suggest many ideas, discuss where additional information could be found. Groups could be assigned to check out the suggested sources.

5. Add advantages and disadvantages to the class list as they are suggested by groups or individual students.

6. Have groups of students or individual students complete **BLM 2.7.4**. Possible responses for this activity can be found on **BLM 2.7.5**.

7. To provide an opportunity to track students' understanding of basic concepts, use the anecdotal record sheet on **BLM 2.UW.2a**. Possible teacher comments are represented on **BLM 2.UW.2b**.

Adaptations
All accommodations must take into account the student's Individual Education Plan. All of the tasks and activities are designed to accommodate the needs of students at different levels of abilities. For detailed strategies see number 9 in the Notes to Teacher section of the Unit Overview.

Resources

	BLM 2.7.1	BLM_7.1.cwk
	BLM 2.7.2	BLM_7.2.cwk
	BLM 2.7.3	BLM_7.3.pdf
	BLM 2.7.4	BLM_7.4.cwk
	BLM 2.7.5	BLM_7.5.cwk
	Energy Forever? Water Power	Ian Graham

Energy from Wind and Moving Water
Energy and Control An Integrated Unit for Grade 2

Sources of Energy
Subtask 7
60 mins

- **Energy Forever? Wind Power** — Ian Graham
- **Changes in Energy** — Magic Lantern Communications Ltd.
  10 Meteor Drive Toronto, Ontario   M9W 1A4
- crayons
- chart paper
- photographs of wind turbines on a wind farm

Notes to Teacher

Information About Water Power

   Water is an important energy source in Canada as it is used to produce electricity. Almost 60% of the electricity produced in Canada comes from hydroelectric power plants. Hydroelectric power is very clean energy. However, hydroelectric plants are expensive to build.
   Most hydroelectric power plants include two main parts: a dam and a generating station. Huge dams are built to create lakes called reservoirs. The dam holds the water in place so that it has gravitational energy (the water behind the dam is higher than the turbines). The generating station consists of a number of turbines. Turbines are specially designed large wheels. As water flows through the turbines, the water causes the turbines to spin. This transforms the water's gravitational energy into kinetic energy. The turbines are connected to a generator that transforms the kinetic energy into electrical energy. This electrical energy is carried by power lines to where it is needed.

Teacher Reflections

Energy from Wind and Moving Water
Energy and Control An Integrated Unit for Grade 2

Summative Task
Subtask 8
300 mins

Description
Students will design and build a device to transport a load across water. The device must be powered by water or air. After testing the device and making the necessary modifications, students will demonstrate the effectiveness of their device and explain how the device was constructed.

Expectations

2s49	• demonstrate an understanding of the movement of air and of water as sources of energy;
2s50	• design and construct devices that are propelled by moving air or moving water;
2s51	• identify wind and moving water as renewable sources of energy and determine the advantages and disadvantages of using them.
2s57	– ask questions about and identify needs and problems related to the use of wind and moving water as energy sources, and explore possible answers and solutions (e.g., describe how moving water is used to produce electricity; describe how windmills were used to grind grain into flour);
2s58	– plan investigations to answer some of these questions or solve some of these problems, and describe the steps involved;
2s59	– use appropriate vocabulary in describing their investigations, explorations, and observations (e.g., use terms such as renewable and movement when describing energy);
2s60	– record relevant observations, findings, and measurements, using written language, pictures, and charts (e.g., draw a diagram of their device; prepare a chart to present data on the distance travelled by their device over time);
2s61	– communicate the procedures and results of investigations and explorations for specific purposes, using drawings, demonstrations, and oral and written descriptions (e.g., prepare a showcase of different devices that are propelled by wind energy; explain the effect of wind direction and speed on the displacement of wind-propelled devices).

Groupings
Students Working In Small Groups
Students Working Individually
Students Working As A Whole Class

Teaching / Learning Strategies
Collaborative/cooperative Learning
Learning Log/ Journal
Oral Explanation
Rehearsal / Repetition / Practice
Model Making

Assessment

Assessment Strategies
Performance Task
Classroom Presentation
Learning Log
Self Assessment

Assessment Recording Devices
Rubric
Checklist

Teaching / Learning
Part A: Design and Build

1. Set the scene by bringing in some camping gear (e.g. knapsack, sleeping bag, flashlight). Draw an island on the board. Set a fan blowing toward the drawing of the island. Gather students around in a group to read the story of *The Lighthouse Keeper's Lunch*. Ask students if they have ever been on a camping trip. Brainstorm a list of things they would need to take on a camping trip.

2. Present the following context and description of the performance task to the students:
"You and your friends are going on a camping trip to an island with a steady, strong wind coming on-shore. You must get your friends, yourself and your camping gear across to the island without getting wet. Before leaving home, you must create a model of a transportation device in order to test its effectiveness. Your device must be powered by water or air." Explain to students that they must design and build a device

Energy from Wind and Moving Water
Energy and Control An Integrated Unit for Grade 2

Summative Task
Subtask 8
300 mins

capable of transporting a load of at least 10 pennies across water. When they have finished building and testing their device, they demonstrate and explain how the device operates as well as describe how it was constructed.

3. Review the devices propelled by air and water which have been investigated throughout this unit (i.e., air devices such as hovercraft, sails, land rover, pinwheel and water devices such as water-powered paddles).

4. Review the S.P.I.C.E. Model chart which was initiated in Subtask 1 (see S.P.I.C.E. Model on **BLM 2.UW.4**). Explain to students that their device will be assessed according to its ability to carry a load (pennies) over a distance and the time it takes to travel the required distance. These criteria should be posted on a chart for reference throughout the summative task. Discuss the Wind/ Water Powered Device Rubric (see **BLM 2.8.6**) which will be used to evaluate the devices.

5. Create groups of three or four students. In these groups, students will discuss possible devices which could be used to solve the problem.

6. After this discussion, each student will create a simple design or blueprint of his/her device using **BLM 2.8.1**. When the designs have been completed, students will decide on the appropriate tools and materials to use when constructing their device. These will be recorded on **BLM 2.8.2** and as students construct their device, they record the steps taken and the changes made after testing. It is essential that students are given opportunities to test their device in water in order to make necessary modifications.

7. To test the devices, set up a long wallpaper tray or a child's swimming pool filled with water, located on the floor of the classroom. Have a fan available to blow across the surface of the water for those students who choose to design a craft using air. The same set-up should be used for the final demonstration.

Part B: Demonstrating and Assessing

1. When students have completed their devices, they record in their science and technology journals how their device was constructed, its energy input and how well it performed. This information helps students prepare for their class presentation. Journal entries can be assessed using the journal writing rubric on **BLM 2.UW.9**.

2. In their oral presentations, students explain how the device was constructed. They demonstrate how their device can travel across water as well as carry a load. Ten pennies should be used as the load so that all students use the same objects ("fair test"). The teacher should ask each student where the pennies should be placed. Distance travelled should be measured. Data is compiled in a class chart with the following headings: DEVICE, ENERGY SOURCE, LOAD, DISTANCE TRAVELLED. Students complete the "Demonstrating" section of **BLM 2.8.3.**

3. Students engage in a class discussion about what they have learned about wind and water energy and the construction of effective devices.

4. As a final evaluation, students should complete Part 2 - Assessing Learned Knowledge on **BLM 2.1.3**. They also complete the Self-Assessment for Wind/Water Propelled Device on **BLM 2.8.7**. These sheets can be sent home with other work on this unit to provide information to parents/guardians concerning their child's progress.

Adaptations

All accommodations must take into account the student's Individual Education Plan. All of the tasks and activities are designed to accommodate the needs of students at different levels of abilities. For detailed strategies see

Energy from Wind and Moving Water
Energy and Control An Integrated Unit for Grade 2

Summative Task
Subtask 8
300 mins

number 9 in the Notes to Teacher section of the Unit Overview.

Resources

- BLM 2.8.1 — BLM_8.1.cwk
- BLM 2.8.2 — BLM_8.2.cwk
- BLM 2.8.3 — BLM_8.3.cwk
- BLM 2.8.4 — BLM_8.4.cwk
- BLM 2.8.5 — BLM_8.5.cwk
- BLM 2.8.6 — BLM_8.6.cwk
- BLM 2.8.7 — BLM_8.7.cwk
- The Lighthouse Keepers Lunch — Penguin Books
- assortment of paper
- masking tape
- duct tape
- elastics
- white glue and carpenter's glue
- modelling clay
- styrofoam trays
- cardboard boxes
- plastic containers and lids
- large and small straws
- wooden stir sticks
- paper towel rolls
- plastic wrap and tin foil
- lightweight fabric
- non-latex balloons

Energy from Wind and Moving Water
Energy and Control An Integrated Unit for Grade 2

Summative Task
Subtask 8
300 mins

- wooden barbeque skewers
- film canisters
- corks
- Jinks wood mitre boxes
- scissors
- cold temperature glue gun
- hair dryer or fan
- junior hacksaws
- mitre boxes
- measuring tapes
- water table or child's plastic swimming pool
- pennies for the load

Notes to Teacher

Teacher Reflections

Appendices
Energy from Wind and Moving Water
Energy and Control

Resource List:

Black Line Masters:

Rubrics:

Unit Expectation List and Expectation Summary:

Energy from Wind and Moving Water
Energy and Control An Integrated Unit for Grade 2

Resource List
Page 1

Blackline Master / File

☐ **BLM 2.uw.1** BLM_UW.1.cwk	Unit	
☐ **BLM 2.uw.2a** BLM_UW.2a.cwk	Unit	
☐ **BLM 2.uw.2b** BLM_UW.2b.cwk	Unit	
☐ **BLM 2.uw.3** BLM_UW.3.cwk	Unit	
☐ **BLM 2.uw.3a** BLM_UW.3a.cwk	Unit	
☐ **BLM 2.uw.4** BLM_UW.4.cwk	Unit	
☐ **BLM 2.uw.5** BLM_UW.5.cwk	Unit	
☐ **BLM 2.uw.6** BLM_UW.6.pdf	Unit	
☐ **BLM 2.uw.7** BLM_UW.7.cwk	Unit	
☐ **BLM 2.uw.8** BLM_UW.8.cwk	Unit	
☐ **BLM 2.uw.9** BLM_UW.9.cwk	Unit	
☐ **BLM 2.1.1** BLM_1.1.cwk	ST 1	
☐ **BLM 2.1.2** BLM_1.2.cwk	ST 1	
☐ **BLM 2.1.3a** BLM_1.3a.cwk	ST 1	
☐ **BLM 2.1.3b** BLM_1.3b.cwk	ST 1	
☐ **BLM 2.2.1** BLM_2.1.cwk	ST 2	
☐ **BLM 2.2.2** BLM_2.2.cwk	ST 2	
☐ **BLM 2.3.1** BLM_3.1.cwk	ST 3	
☐ **BLM 2.3.2** BLM_3.2.pdf	ST 3	
☐ **BLM 2.3.3** BLM_3.3.cwk	ST 3	
☐ **BLM 2.3.4** BLM_3.4.cwk	ST 3	
☐ **BLM 2.3.5** BLM_3.5.cwk	ST 3	
☐ **BLM 2.3.6** BLM_3.6.cwk	ST 3	
☐ **BLM 2.3.7** BLM_3.7.cwk	ST 3	

☐ **BLM 2.4.1** BLM_4.1.cwk	ST 4
☐ **BLM 2.4.2** BLM_4.2.cwk	ST 4
☐ **BLM 2.4.3** BLM_4.3.cwk	ST 4
☐ **BLM 2.4.4** BLM_4.4.cwk	ST 4
☐ **BLM 2.4.5** BLM_4.5.pdf	ST 4
☐ **BLM 2.4.6** BLM_4.6.cwk	ST 4
☐ **BLM 2.5.1** BLM_5.1.cwk	ST 5
☐ **BLM 2.5.2** BLM_5.2.cwk	ST 5
☐ **BLM 2.5.3a** BLM_5.3a.cwk	ST 5
☐ **BLM 2.5.3b** BLM_5.3b.cwk	ST 5
☐ **BLM 2.6.1** BLM_6.1.cwk	ST 6
☐ **BLM 2.6.2** BLM_6.2.cwk	ST 6
☐ **BLM 2.6.3** BLM_6.3.cwk	ST 6
☐ **BLM 2.7.1** BLM_7.1.cwk	ST 7
☐ **BLM 2.7.2** BLM_7.2.cwk	ST 7
☐ **BLM 2.7.3** BLM_7.3.pdf	ST 7
☐ **BLM 2.7.4** BLM_7.4.cwk	ST 7
☐ **BLM 2.7.5** BLM_7.5.cwk	ST 7
☐ **BLM 2.8.1** BLM_8.1.cwk	ST 8
☐ **BLM 2.8.2** BLM_8.2.cwk	ST 8
☐ **BLM 2.8.3** BLM_8.3.cwk	ST 8
☐ **BLM 2.8.4** BLM_8.4.cwk	ST 8
☐ **BLM 2.8.5** BLM_8.5.cwk	ST 8
☐ **BLM 2.8.6** BLM_8.6.cwk	ST 8
☐ **BLM 2.8.7** BLM_8.7.cwk	ST 8

Energy from Wind and Moving Water
Energy and Control An Integrated Unit for Grade 2

Resource List
Page 2

Print

- **Energy Forever? Water Power** — ST 2
  Ian Graham
  ISBN 0-8172-5363-7
  Raintree Steck-Vaughn Publishers
  Austin, Texas

- **Energy Forever? Water Power** — ST 4
  Ian Graham
  ISBN 0-8172-5363-7

- **Energy Forever? Water Power** — ST 6
  Ian Graham
  ISBN 0-8172-5363-7

- **Energy Forever? Water Power** — ST 7
  Ian Graham
  ISBN 0-8172-5363-7

- **Energy Forever? Wind Power** — ST 2
  Ian Graham
  ISBN 0-8172-5364-5
  Raintree Steck-Vaughn Publishers
  Austin, Texas

- **Energy Forever? Wind Power** — ST 3
  Ian Graham
  ISBN 0-8172-5364-5

- **Energy Forever? Wind Power** — ST 5
  Ian Graham
  ISBN 0-8172-5364-5

- **Energy Forever? Wind Power** — ST 7
  Ian Graham
  ISBN 0-8172-5364-5

- **The Lighthouse Keepers Lunch** — ST 8
  Penquin Books
  ISBN 0140503277

Media

- **Changes in Energy** — ST 7
  Magic Lantern Communications Ltd.
  10 Meteor Drive Toronto, Ontario M9W 1A4

  10 minutes in length

- **Look Again 1 - Sense of Sound** — ST 1
  National Film Board of Canada - Program Sales
  150 John Street Toronto, Ontario M5V 3C3
  Watch the first part of the video called "Between the Walls."

Material

- 1 litre milk cartons cut in half lengthwise — ST 6
- 2 L ice cream containers — ST 4
- assortment of paper — ST 8
- balloons — ST 6
- cardboard boxes — ST 8
- chart paper — ST 1
- chart paper — ST 3
- chart paper — ST 4
- chart paper — ST 7
- clothespin — ST 1
- construction paper — ST 5
- cork with a hole through the middle — ST 1
- corks — ST 8
- crayons — ST 3
- crayons — ST 7
- crayons for colouring the pinwheel — ST 5
- duct tape — ST 4
- duct tape — ST 6
- duct tape — ST 8
- elastics — ST 8
- empty juice boxes — ST 2
- film canisters — ST 8
- Jinks wood — ST 5
- Jinks wood mitre boxes — ST 8
- jug of coloured water — ST 4
- large and small straws — ST 8
- lightweight fabric — ST 8
- liquid soap — ST 1
- long container of water (wallpaper tray) — ST 2
- masking tape — ST 6

Energy from Wind and Moving Water
Energy and Control An Integrated Unit for Grade 2

Resource List
Page 3

☐ masking tape	ST 8
☐ modelling clay	ST 8
☐ non-latex balloons	ST 8
☐ one balloon	ST 1
☐ one inch nails	ST 5
☐ paper clips	ST 5
☐ paper towel rolls	ST 8
☐ pencils	ST 4
☐ plastic containers and lids	ST 8
☐ plastic cups	ST 2
☐ plastic film canisters	ST 4
☐ plastic lids per person	ST 4
☐ plastic or tin containers of different shapes	ST 6
☐ plastic wrap and tin foil	ST 8
☐ plasticine	ST 6
☐ small objects	ST 4
☐ stiff cardboard or plastic margarine lid	ST 1
☐ straws	ST 4
☐ straws	ST 6
☐ string	ST 3
☐ styrofoam trays	ST 8
☐ tape	ST 3
☐ tape	ST 4
☐ thread	ST 4
☐ thread	ST 5
☐ tissue paper	ST 5
☐ toy boats or ping pong balls	ST 2
☐ variety of devices (fan, clock, spring toy, beater)	ST 2
☐ various kinds of fabric	ST 5
☐ water	ST 6
☐ water in jugs	ST 5
☐ white glue and carpenter's glue	ST 8
☐ wooden barbecue skewers	ST 4
☐ wooden barbeque skewers	ST 8
☐ wooden stir sticks	ST 8

Equipment / Manipulative

☐ awl for punching holes	ST 4
☐ bicycle pump or ball pump	ST 6
☐ cold temperature glue gun	ST 8
☐ cups for pouring water	ST 4
☐ deflated ball	ST 6
☐ flexible tubing and valves	ST 6
☐ hair dryer or fan	ST 8
☐ hammer, nails and goggles for punching holes	ST 6
☐ junior hacksaws	ST 8
☐ large plastic basins or a sink	ST 6
☐ measuring tapes	ST 8
☐ mitre boxes	ST 8
☐ oscillating fan	ST 3
☐ pennies for the load	ST 8
☐ photographs of wind turbines on a wind farm	ST 7
☐ pictures of still water and Niagara Falls	ST 4
☐ rubber stopper	ST 6
☐ scissors	ST 8
☐ scissors for punching holes	ST 6
☐ stopwatches	ST 5
☐ water jug	ST 6
☐ water paddles from Subtask 4	ST 5
☐ water table or child's plastic swimming pool	ST 8
☐ woodwind or brass musical instruments	ST 6

Letter to Parents

Dear Parents,

We are about to begin a new science unit called "Energy from Wind and Water." During this unit, the students will be investigating the energy produced from moving air and moving water. Students will be creating simple devices that can be controlled by wind water. For the culminating activity students will design and build a device to transport a load across water as quickly as possible. The device must be powered by air.

Some of the classroom activities use a variety of household items. Please help us in gathering the following items: ping pong balls, wall paper trays, small sections of eaves trough, empty film canisters, duct tape, large corks, plastic lids (e.g. margarine containers), 1 litre milk cartons, apple juice cans, 2 litre ice cream buckets and regular sized straws. As we progress with the unit, please encourage your children to share their ideas and explain the process through which they are working.

Thank you so much for your interest in our new unit.

Sincerely,

DIRECTIONS MAKING THE "HOVERCRAFT"

1. Cut a rectangular piece of stiff cardboard (approx. 10 cm by 16 cm) or use a round plastic lid. If you use the cardboard, round the end of one of the 10 cm sides. Make a small hole in the centre of the cardboard or plastic lid.

2. Make a hole in the centre of the cork. Glue the cork directly over the hole in the cardboard or hole in the plastic lid.

3. Blow up the balloon. Place a clothespin over the narrow end of the balloon so that no air escapes.

4. Put the mouth of the balloon over the cork. The clothespin should remain in place until you are ready to demonstrate the "hovercraft" to the students.

5. Paint the bottom of the cardboard or plastic lid with undiluted liquid soap.

6. Remove the clothespin and watch the vehicle move. If it does not move, it may need a little push to take off.

7. Blow up the balloon again and repeat the demonstration in water. This will work better if the device is constructed from thick, coated cardboard or a plastic lid as these materials will repel the water.

Name: _____

PART 1   ASSESSING PRIOR KNOWLEDGE

Tell what you know about...

Energy	Air	Water

BLM 2.1.3a

Name: _____

PART 2   ASSESSING KNOWLEDGE

Tell everything you learned about...

Energy	Air	Water

BLM 2.1.3b

CHALLENGE #1 - TASK CARD

Can you make a plastic cup move without touching it?

Materials you will use: - plastic cup
 - empty juice box

Think About:

1. Is wind (moving air) a source of energy?

2. How many <u>different</u> ways can you move the cup?

BLM 2.2.1

CHALLENGE #2 - TASK CARD

Can you make an object move across water without touching it?

Materials you may use:
- toy boat or ping pong ball
- wallpaper tray

Think About:

I. Is moving water a source of energy?
II. How many different ways can you move the object across the water?

TEACHER REFERENCE - THE WIND CYCLE

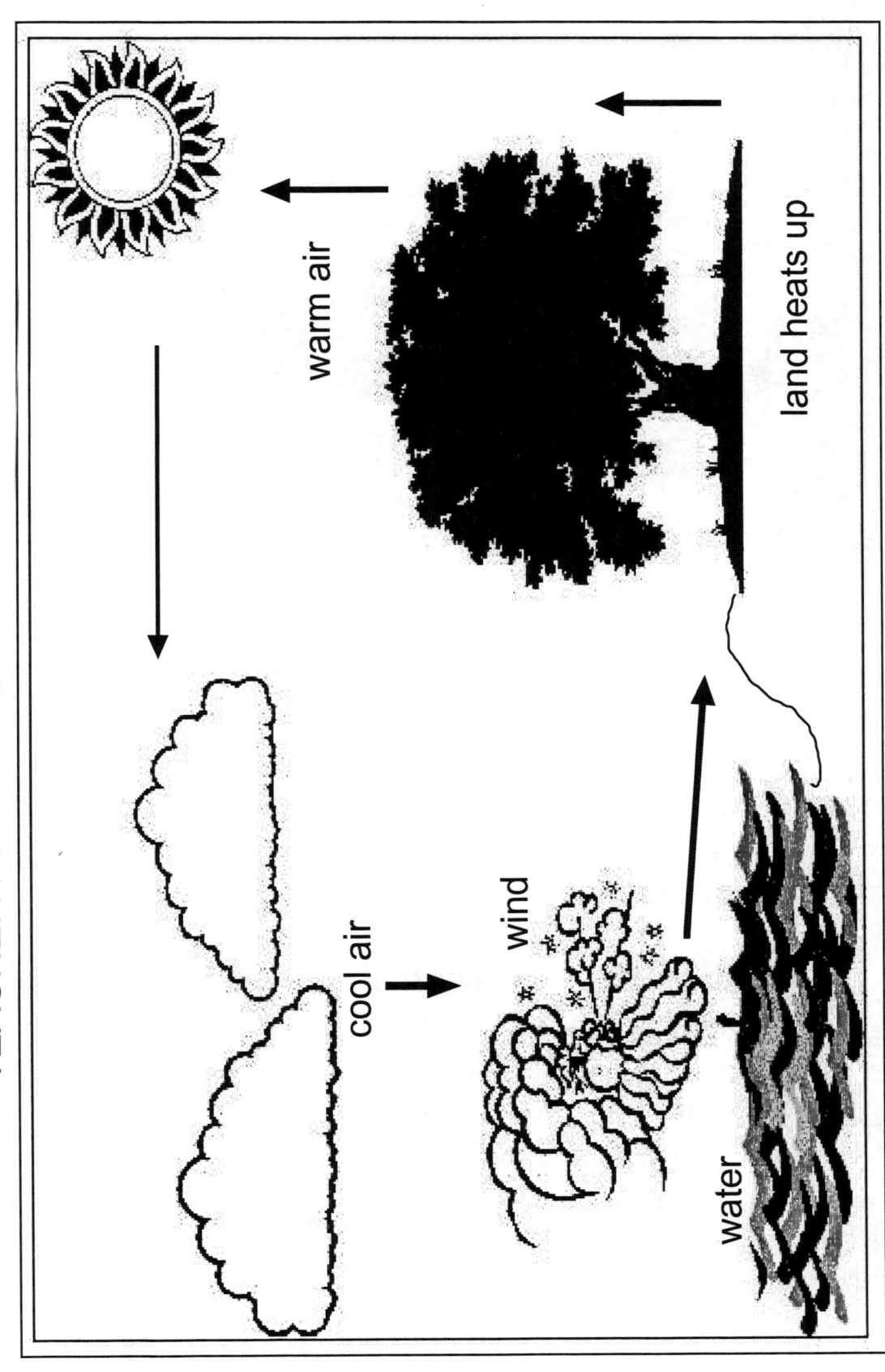

warm air

land heats up

cool air

wind

water

In the Day
- the land will warm up faster than the water
- air at ground level heats up and rises
- cool air moves in to replace the warm air
- the movement of air forms the wind

In the Night
- parts of the land cool off faster than other parts
- parts of the land cool off faster than the water
- the wind blows in the opposite direction

BLM 2.3.1

Name: _____

THE WIND CYCLE AT THE SEASHORE

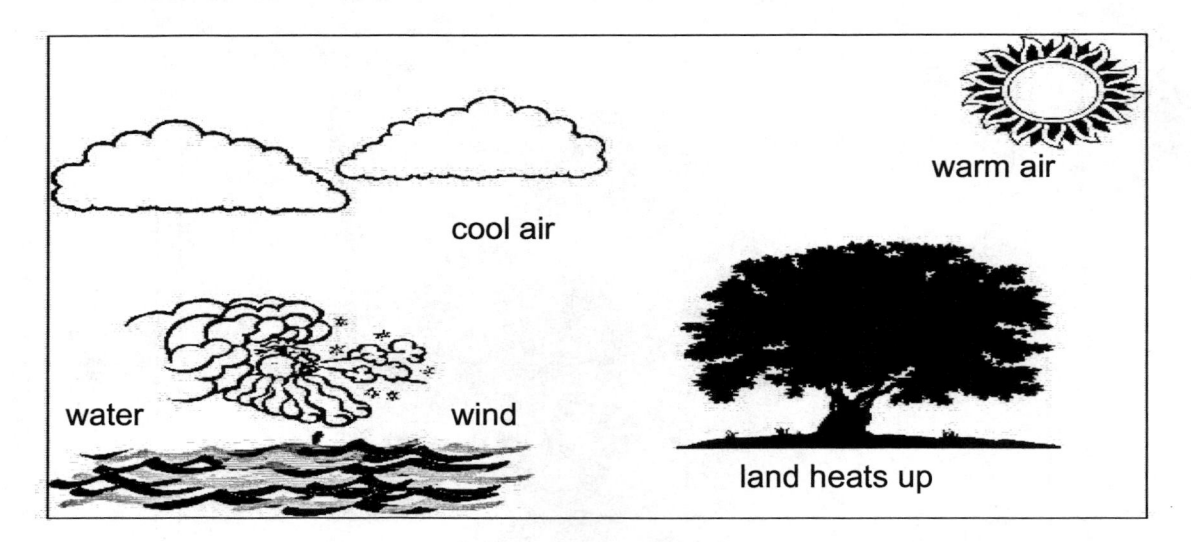

What happens? Use the words below to fill in the blanks.

land   air   warm   cool   rises   wind
water   sun

On a sunny day, the _____ warms the air, the land and the water. The _____ heats up more quickly than the _____. The warm air above the land _____ toward the sun.

The _____ air above the water moves over to replace the warm _____.

The _____ air moves away from the sun and it cools above the water. The movement of the air is the _____.

At night, the land cools more quickly than the water and the wind blows in the opposite direction.

BLM 2.3.2

WIND WIGGLER PATTERN
CIRCULAR SHAPE

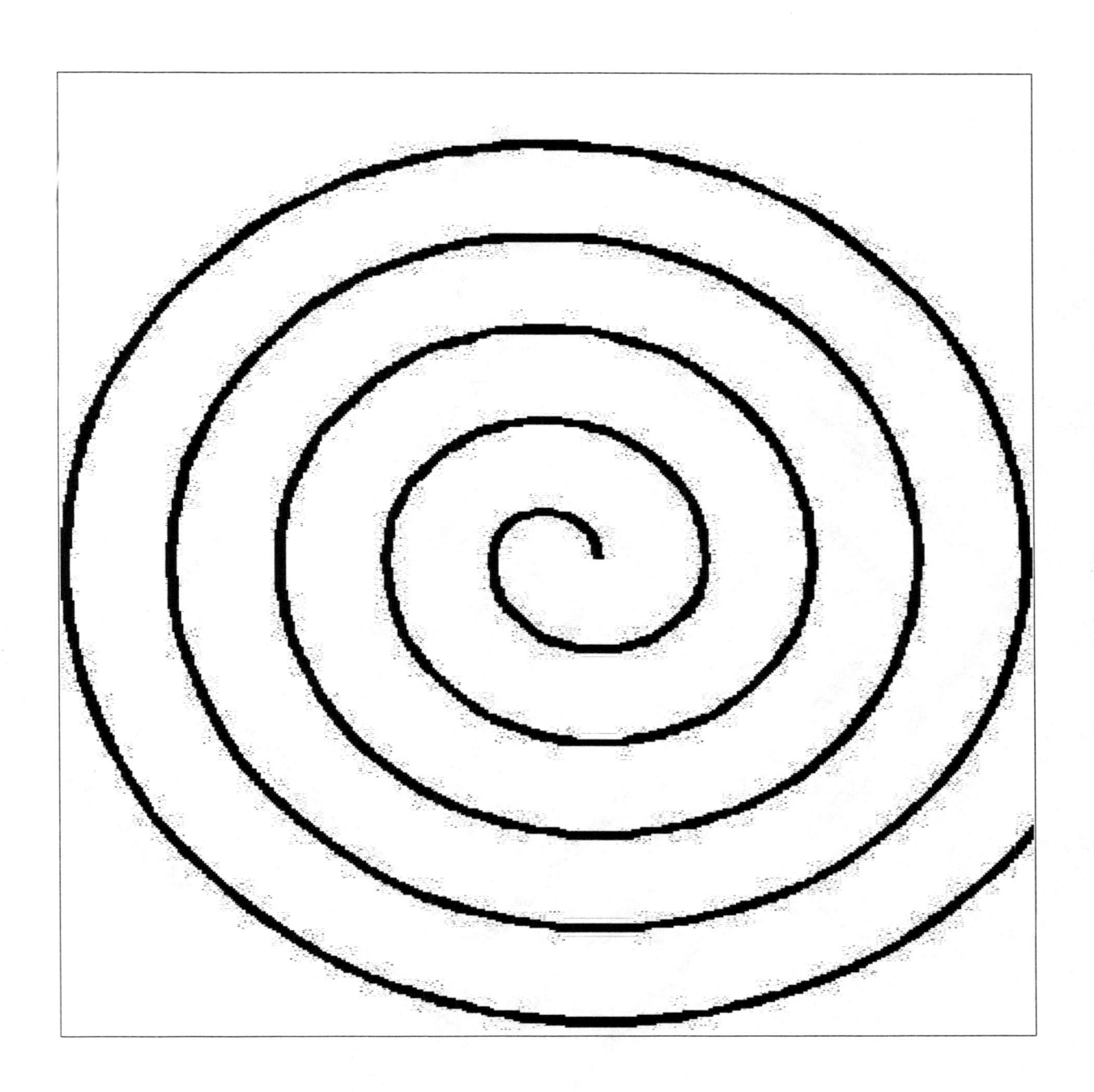

BLM 2.3.3

WIND WIGGLER PATTERN
SQUARE SHAPE

BLM 2.3.4

WIND WIGGLER PATTERN
OVAL SHAPE

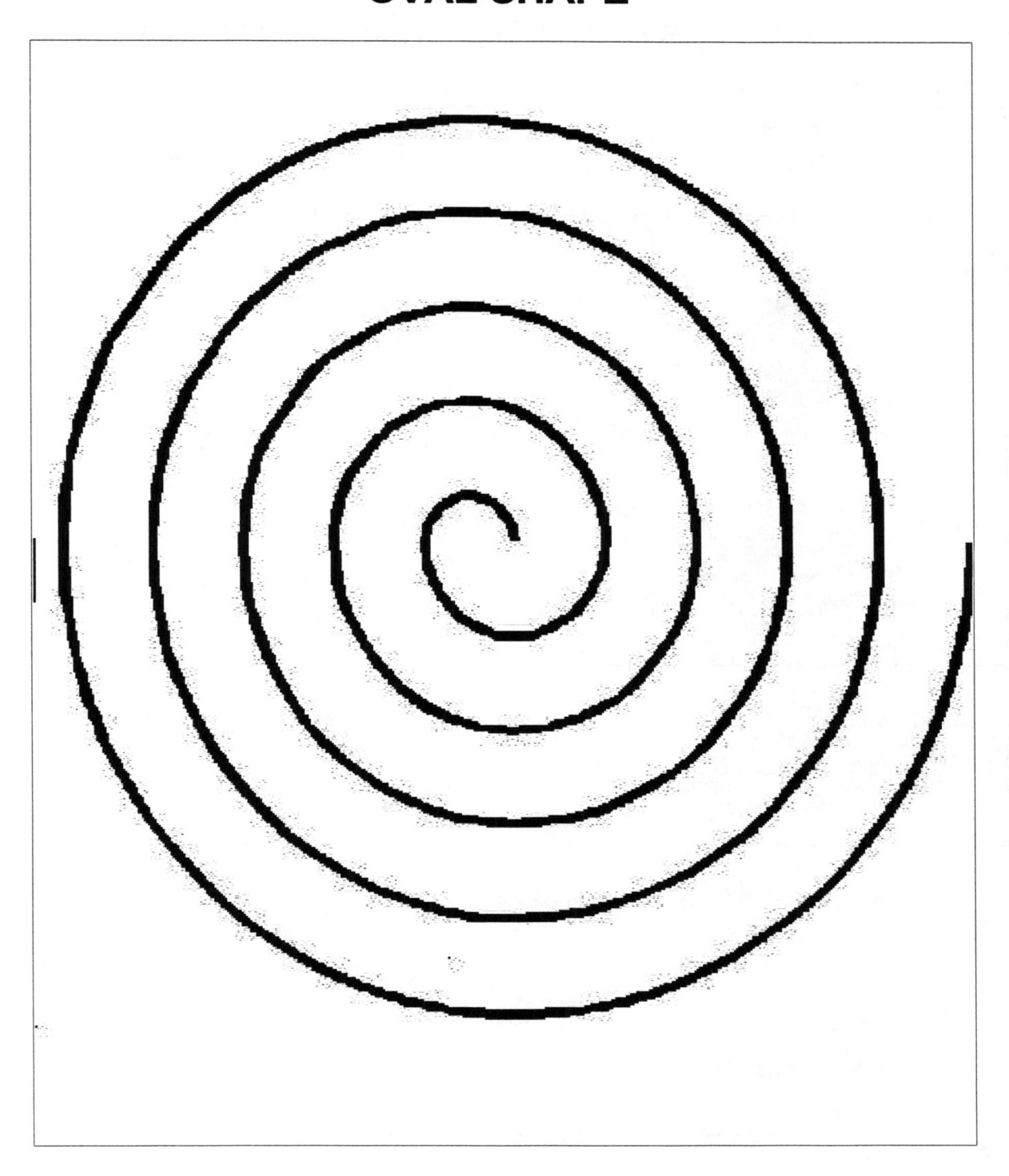

BLM 2.3.5

TESTING WIND WIGGLERS CHART

Type of wind wiggler	Wind wiggler works		
	okay	well	great
spiral			
squal			
oval			

1. What did you learn from doing this experiment?

   _____

   _____

2. Why is one wiggler better than another?

   _____

   _____

BLM 2.3.6

Checklist for Wind Wiggler Activity

Student Name	follows directions accurately	creates 3 working wind wigglers	predicts and gives a reason for prediction	records observation clearly and precisely	experiments why one wind wiggler works better than the other	Comments

WATER WHEEL PATTERN

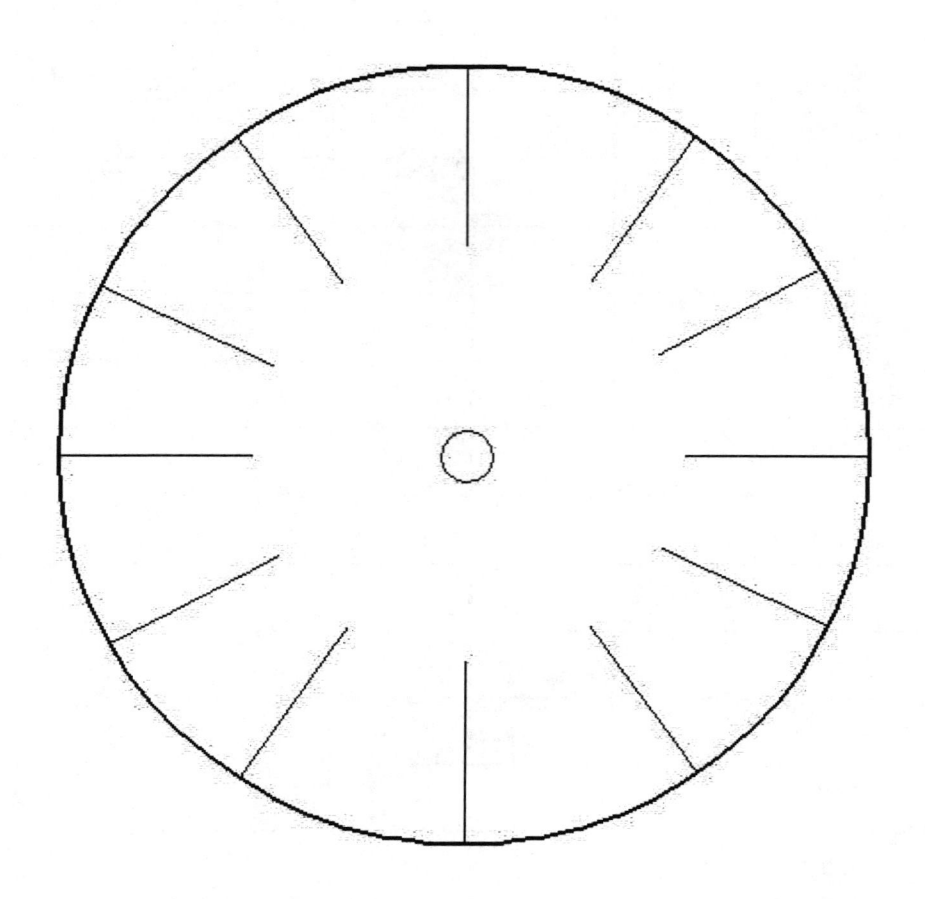

BLM 2.4.1

Name: _____

RECORDING MY OBSERVATIONS ABOUT WATER WHEELS

1. What made the water wheel rotate?

   _____

   _____

   _____

2. What happened to the water wheel when:

Water	Test 1	Test 2	Test 3
water was still (not moving)			
water was moving slowly			
water was moving quickly			

3. What happened when an object was attached to the axle of the water wheel?

   _____

   _____

4. What could you do to improve your water wheel?

   _____

   _____

   _____

BLM 2.4.2

CHECKLIST FOR WATER WHEEL ACTIVITY

Name of Student: _____   Date: _____

Criteria	Yes	No
- follows directions accurately		
- creates a working water wheel		
- experiments constructively with the water wheel		
- works cooperatively with team		
- explains how the water wheel works		
- records observations clearly and precisely		
- generates ideas to make the water wheel more efficient		

Comments:
_____
_____
_____
_____
_____

HOW TO MAKE A WATER PADDLE

Materials Needed:
- plastic film canister or large cork
- 2L ice cream container
- wooden skewer
- cup for water or faucet
- plastic lids
- duct tape
- water
- awl for punching holes

Steps:
1. Draw a cross shape on the bottom of the film canister.
2. Have your teacher make one hole at the top and one hole at the bottom of your film canister.
3. Make holes on opposite sides of your ice cream container, near the top. The holes must be big enough to let the skewer spin freely.
4. Trace this pattern onto the plastic lid four times and then cut out. This will make four blades.

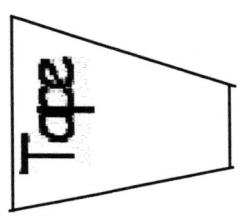

(trapezoid shape labeled "Tape")

5. Attach duct tape to one side of the wide end of the blades. Now attach the blade to the side of the film canister using the cross marks as a guide. Then attach duct tape to the other side of the blade and attach it to the canister.
6. Stick the skewer through the hole on one side of the ice cream container, then through the film canister and finally through the hole on the opposite side of the ice cream container.
7. Test to see if your water paddle can spin freely by turning the skewer with your hand.
8. Use the cup to pour water onto the flaps of the paddle or hold it under the faucet. What happens?

Construction Steps for Making a Water Paddle

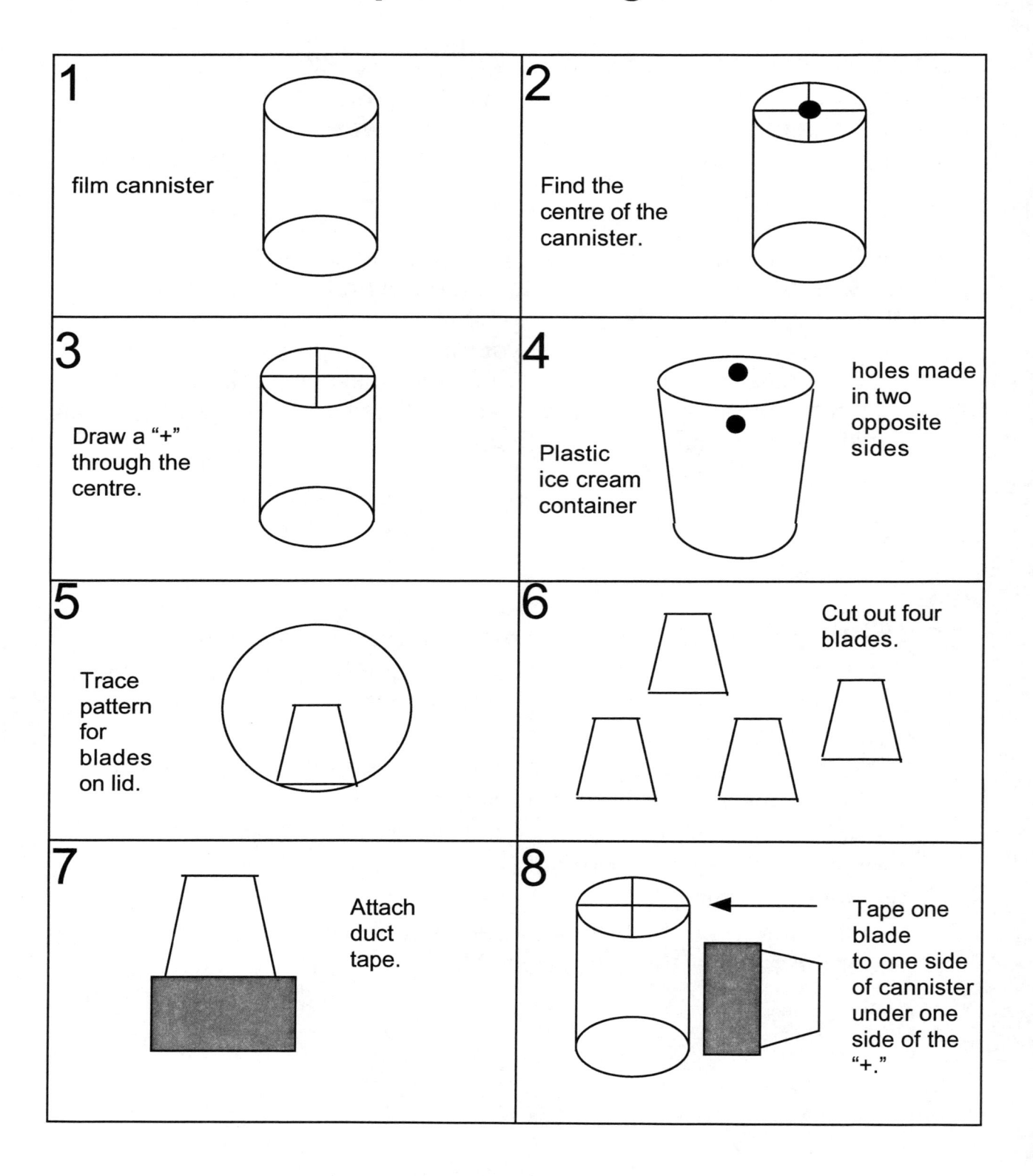

1 film cannister	**2** Find the centre of the cannister.
3 Draw a "+" through the centre.	**4** Plastic ice cream container — holes made in two opposite sides
5 Trace pattern for blades on lid.	**6** Cut out four blades.
7 Attach duct tape.	**8** Tape one blade to one side of cannister under one side of the "+."

BLM 2.4.5

9 Add tape to other side of blade to secure it.

10 Add second blade.

11 Add third blade.

12 Add fourth blade.

13

BLM 2.4.5

Name: _____

EXPERIMENTING WITH MY WATER PADDLE

What happens when water is poured onto the blades of the water paddle?
_____

_____

Height water is poured from:	What happens to the water paddle?
- just above the paddles	
- 15 cm above the paddles	
- 30 cm above the paddles	
- 50 cm above the paddles	

At which water height did the water paddle work the best?

_____

BLM 2.4.6

The Pinwheel

To make the pinwheel follow the steps below. Steps 1 to 4 are steps for the students to do independently. Students will probably require assistance with steps 5 to 7. Step 8 is best done by an adult.

1) Cut a piece of Jinks wood to measure 20 cm in length and make a mark (dot) in the middle of the wood 1 cm from the top.

2) Cut the large square shape (20 cm x 20 cm) from the sheet. Do not cut the diagonal lines at this time.

3) Colour the four quadrants (the areas between the diagonal lines), use a different colour in each quadrant. Repeat the same colouring pattern on the back of the square.

4) Cut the diagonal lines. When the solid line ends, stop cutting. Do not cut all the way from one diagonal line to the other. Do not cut the dashed lines.

5) Carefully bend the flaps into the centre so that the hole marks line up. The four flaps should over lap so you'll only be able to see the top hole mark.

6) Push a 1" common nail through the top hole mark and on through all the flaps and the bottom of the paper pinwheel.

7) Slide the nail back and forth in the hole to expand the size of the hole.

8) Centre the point of the nail on the mark made earlier on the piece of Jinks wood and lightly hammer the nail into the wood. Do not hammer too heavily or you will split the wood. Do not hammer all the way through the wood. The point of the nail should not protrude from the wood. If the nail does protrude from the wood press the wood against a hard surface (metal is best) to force the nail back into the wood.

BLM 2.5.1

Pinwheel Pattern

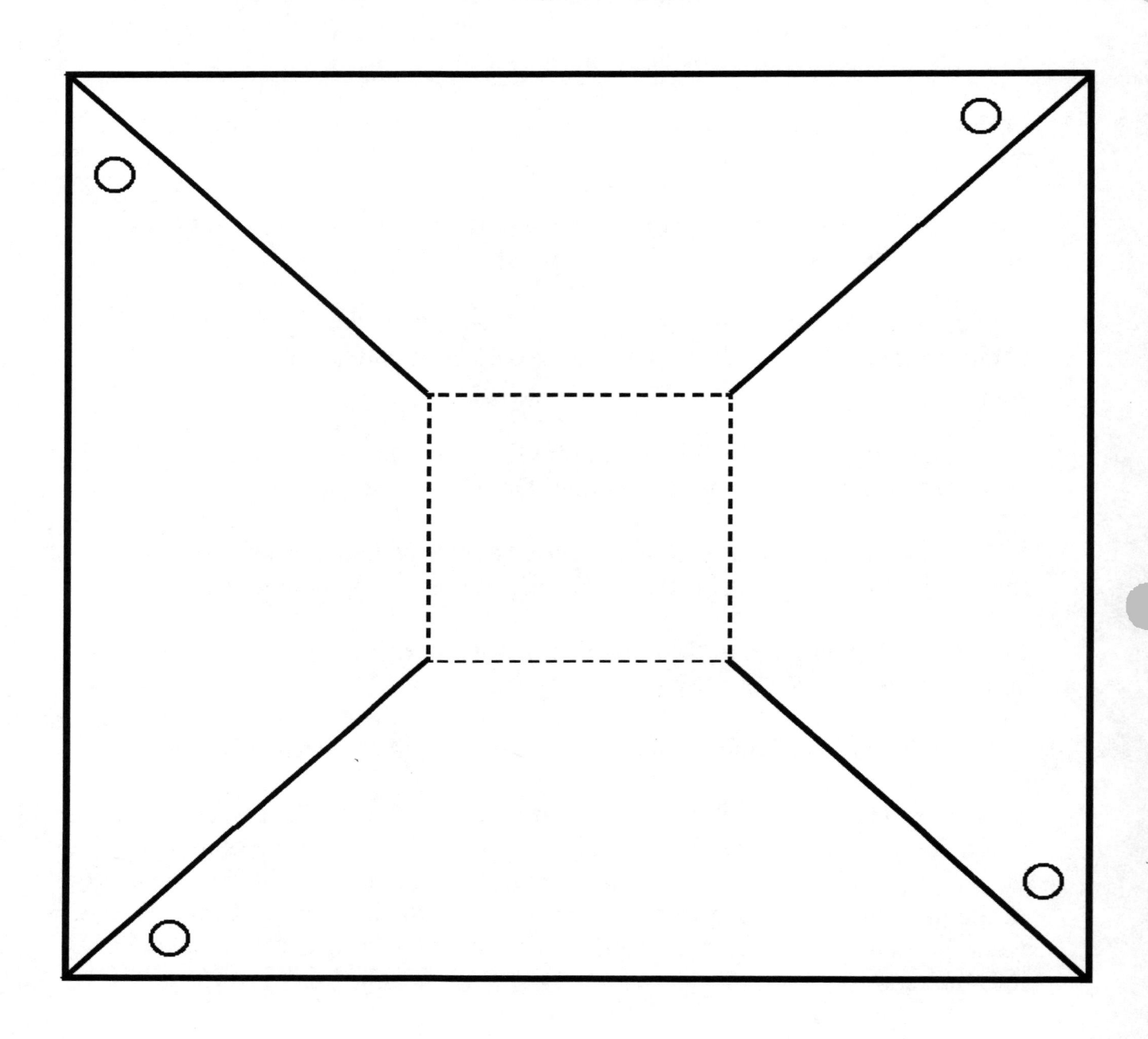

BLM 2.5.2

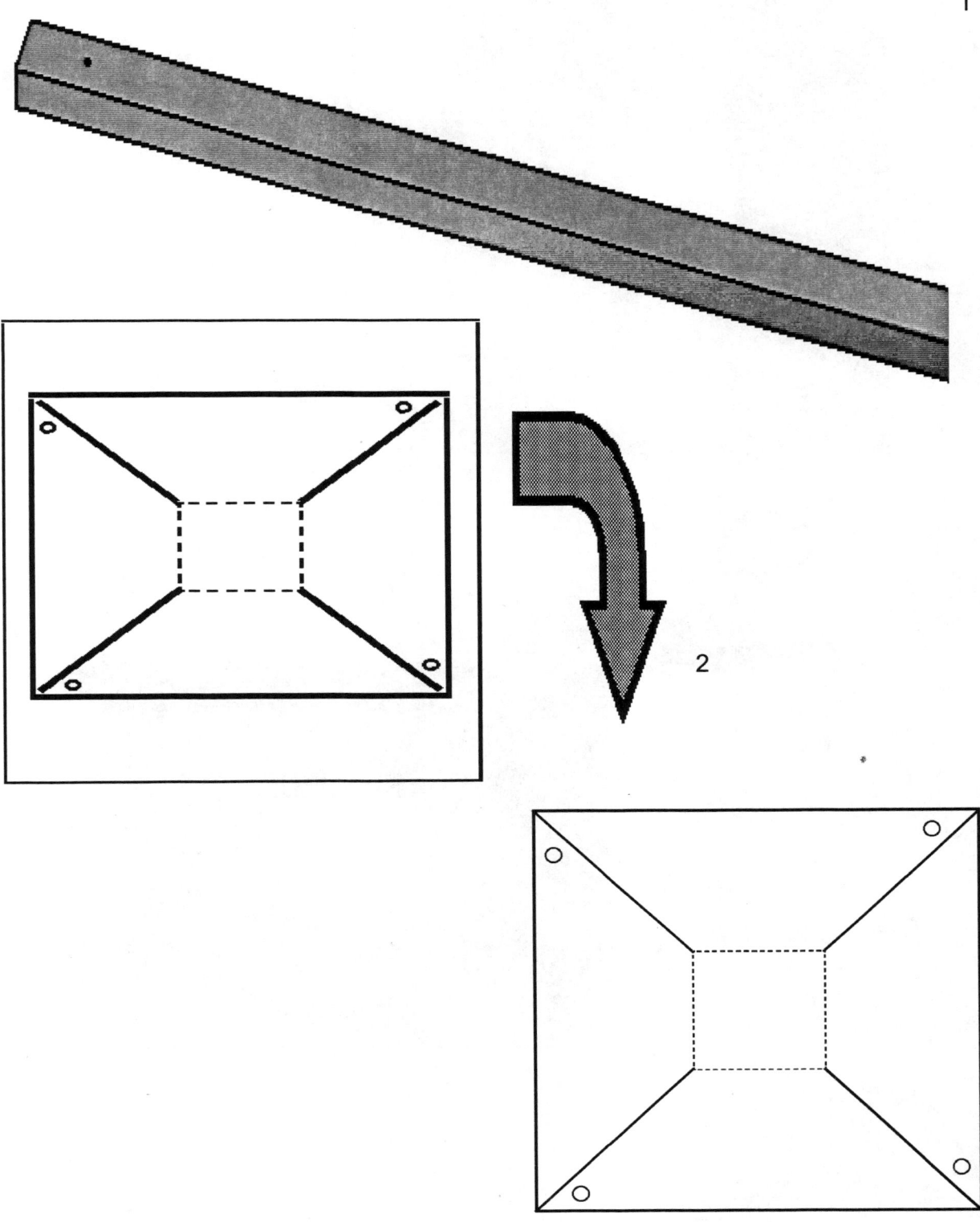

BLM 2.5.2

3

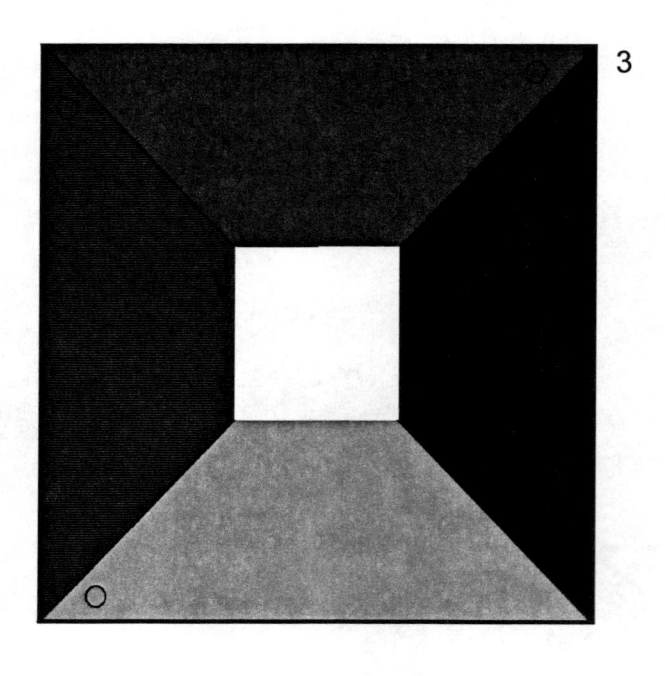

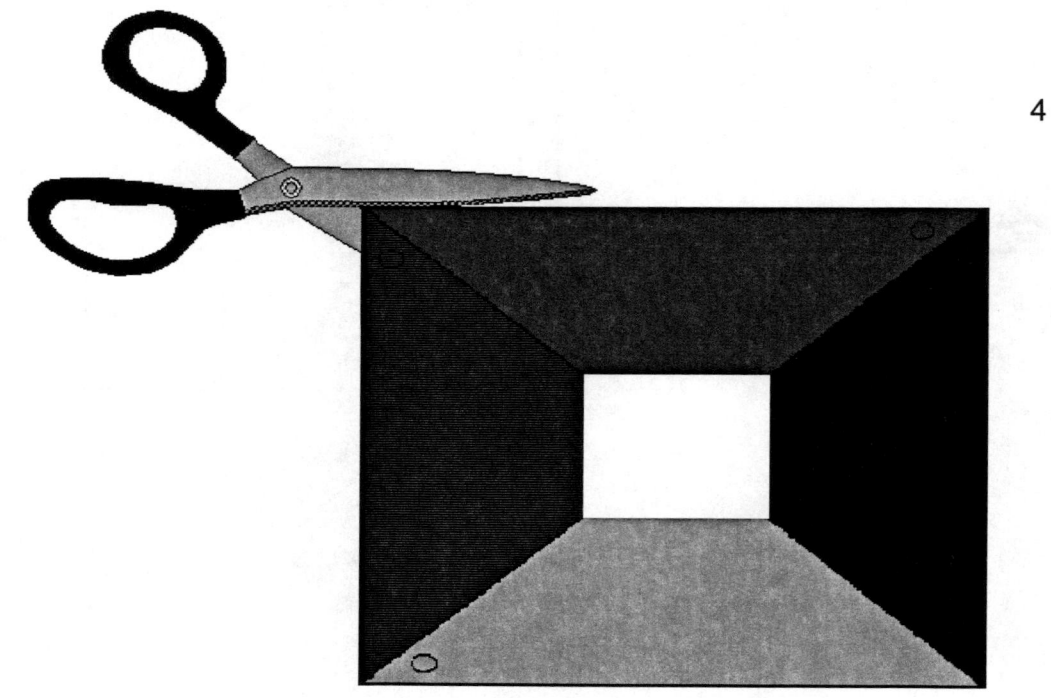

4

5

BLM 2.5.2

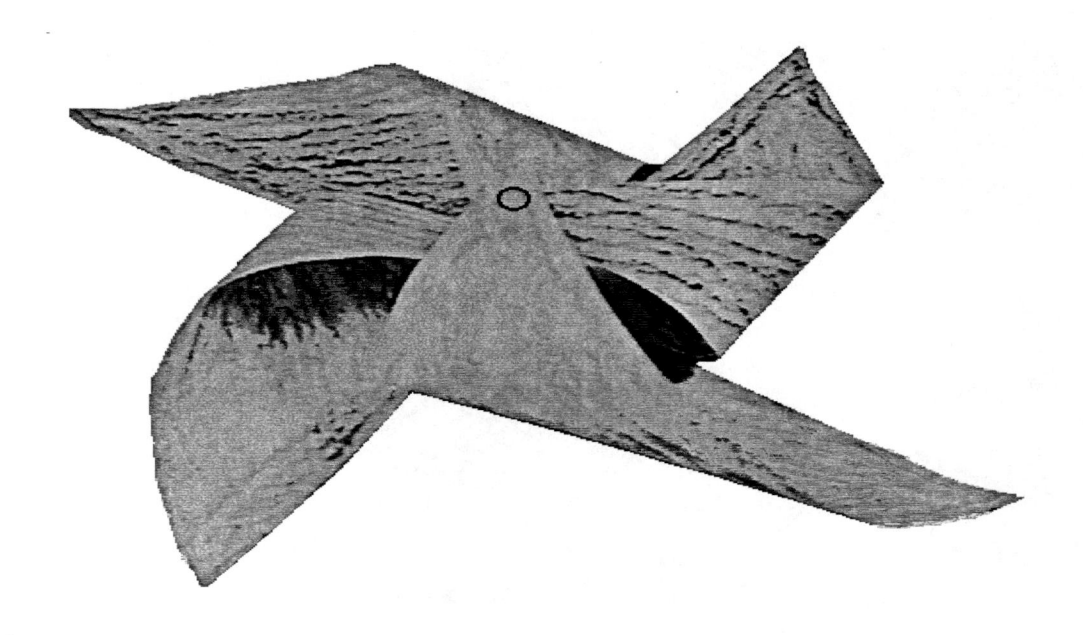

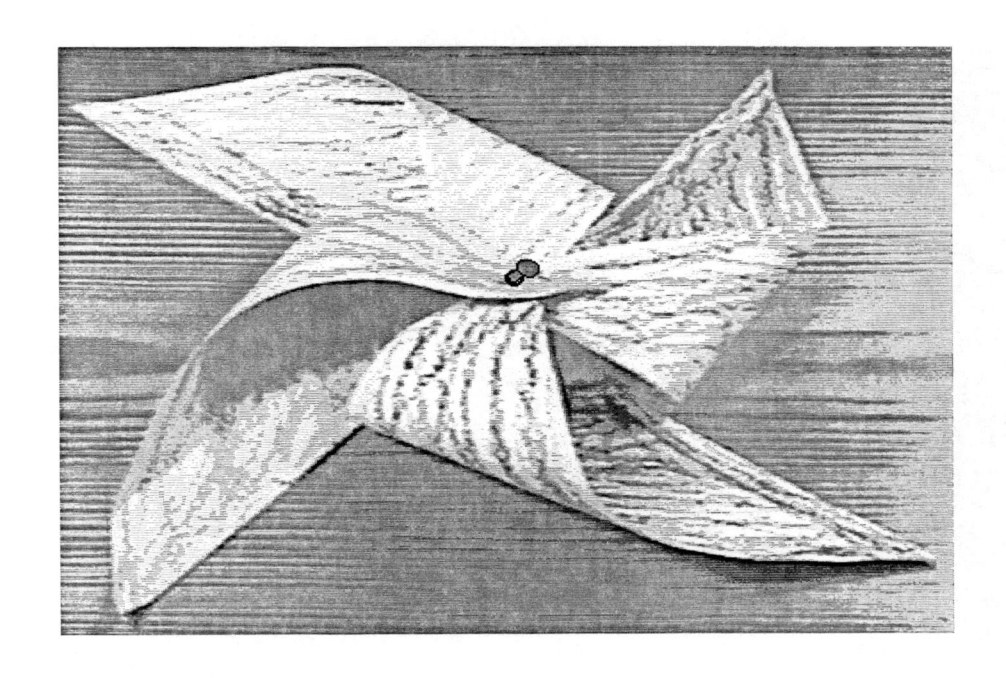

6

7

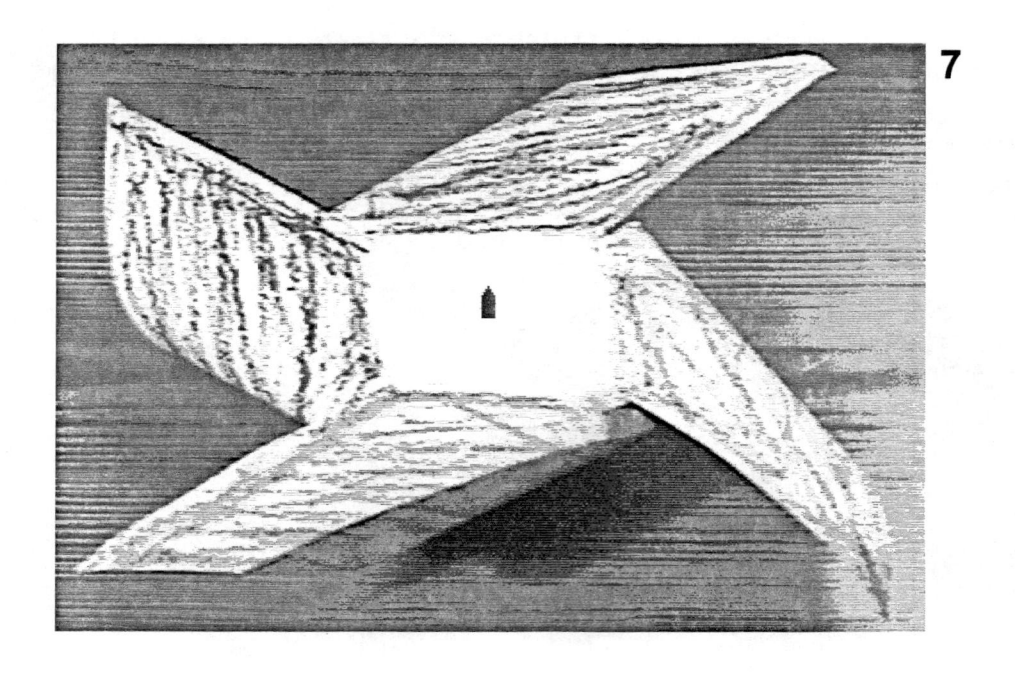

8

BLM 2.5.2

Your finished pinwheel should look like this.

BLM 2.5.2

THE PINWHEEL

Part 1

1. What makes the pinwheel turn?

   _____

   _____

2. How many directions does it turn?

   _____

   _____

3. How can you make it turn faster?

   _____

   _____

4. Why does the pinwheel turn?

   _____

   _____

Part 2

1. How would you change your pinwheel to make it better?

   _____

   _____

   _____

   _____

THE PINWHEEL

Part 1

1. What makes the pinwheel turn?
   The force of the moving air - wind created by blowing on it.

2. How many directions does it turn?
   Two, this depends on the direction of the wind.

I. 3. How can we make it turn faster?
   The wind must be moving faster (blow harder on the blades).
   Hold the pinwheel closer to the wind source (mouth).

4. Why does the pinwheel turn?
   The pinwheel turns because the wind pushes on the blades causing them to move. The nail holds the pinwheel to the wood and as the wind is caught by the blades, they rotate.

Part 2

1. How would you change your pinwheel to make it better?
   Answers will vary. Students may suggest changing the number or size of the sails, the length of the Jinks wood, or correcting any mistakes that they made during construction.

Name: _____

TESTING THE LAND ROVER

Straw Length	My Results	#2's Results	#3's Results
short straw			
medium straw			
long straw			

What length of straw was the best? _____

Why do you think this straw was the best? _____
_____
_____

What length of straw made the air go out the fastest?
_____
_____

What length of straw made the air go out the slowest?
_____

BLM 2.6.1

Name: _____

THE FOUNTAIN CHALLENGE

Group	Distance Water Shot

Which group's fountain made water go the farthest?
_____

How would you change your fountain to make water go farther?

_____

_____

_____

_____

_____

How Would a City Get Its Water?

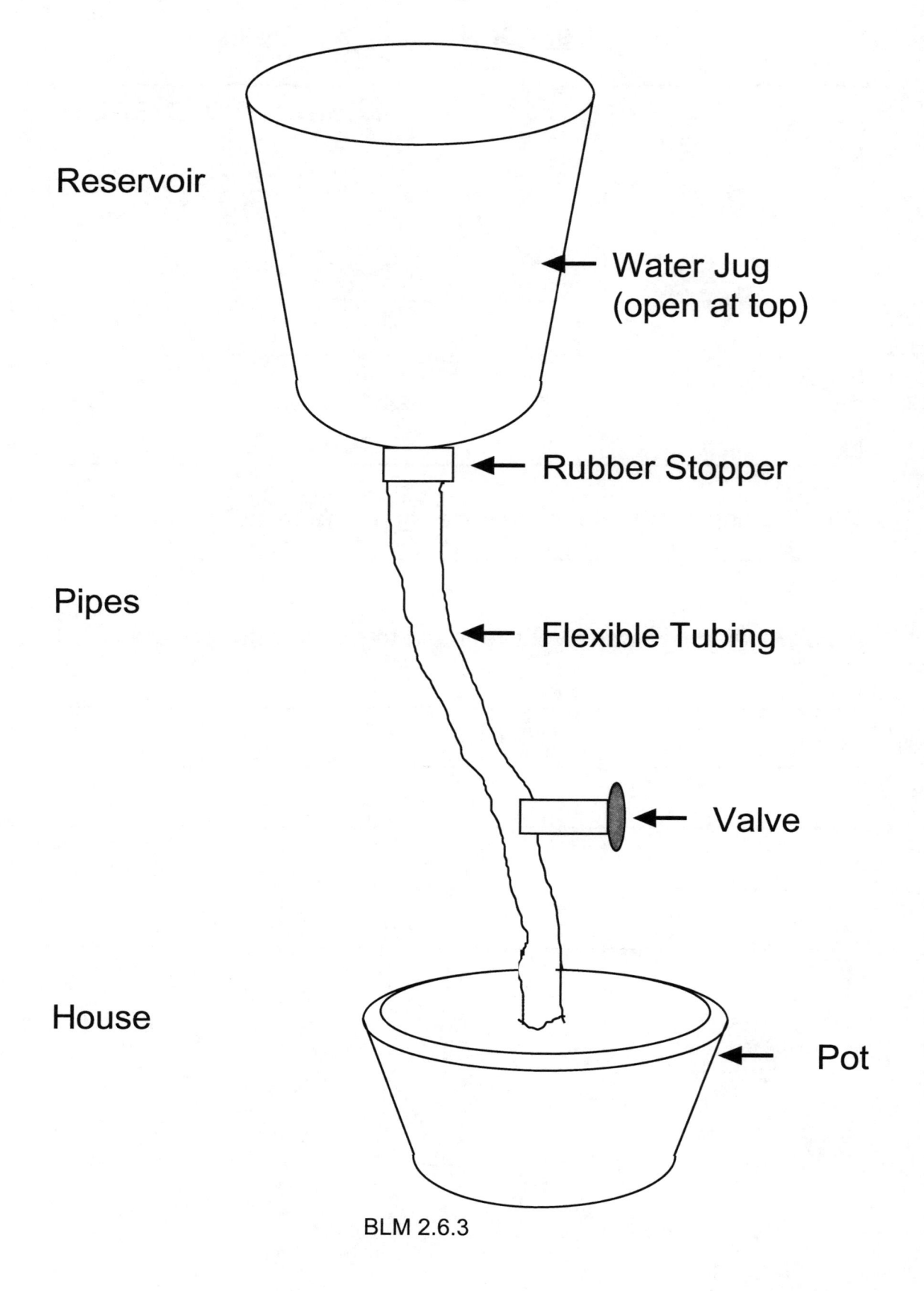

Reservoir ← Water Jug (open at top)

← Rubber Stopper

Pipes ← Flexible Tubing

← Valve

House ← Pot

BLM 2.6.3

Name _____

HOW DO WE GET ELECTRICITY?

Electricity from Moving Water

Falling _____ turns the turbine.

The _____ going around and _____ makes _____

Words

turbine   electricity
around   water

BLM 2.7.1

Name _____

HOW DO WE GET ELECTRICITY?

Electricity from Wind

The _____ makes the _____ blades of the _____ go around. The turbine going around and _____ makes _____.

Words

turbine   electricity
around   water

BLM 2.7.2

Teacher Resource
How Do We Get Electricity

Electricity from Moving Water

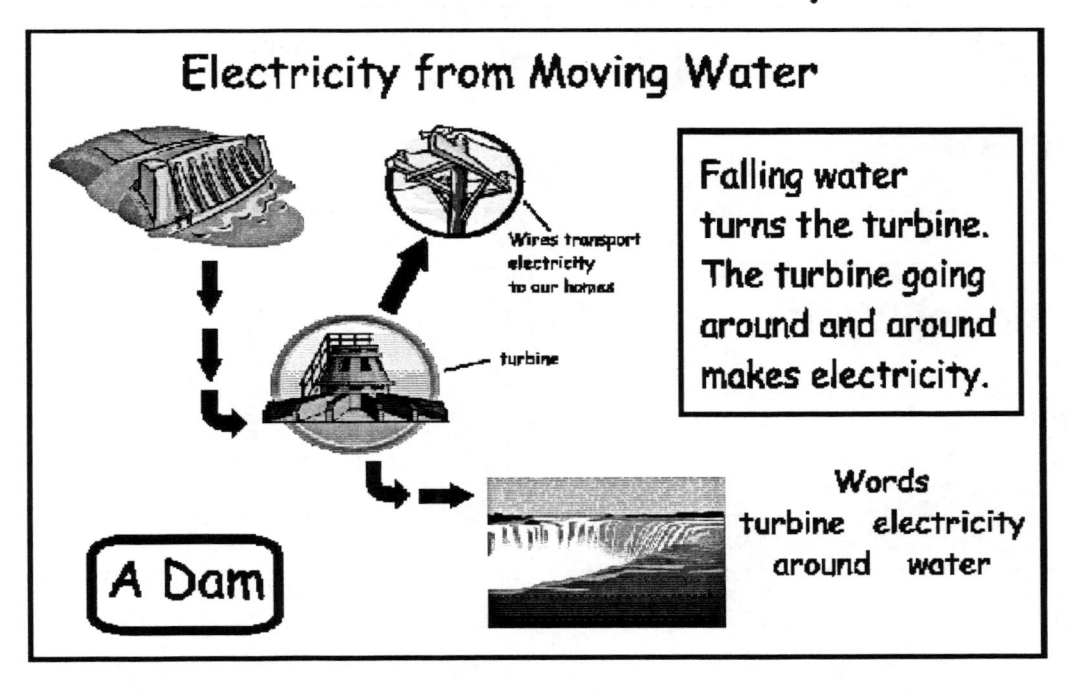

Wires transport electricity to our homes

turbine

A Dam

Falling water turns the turbine. The turbine going around and around makes electricity.

Words
turbine   electricity
around   water

Electricity from Wind

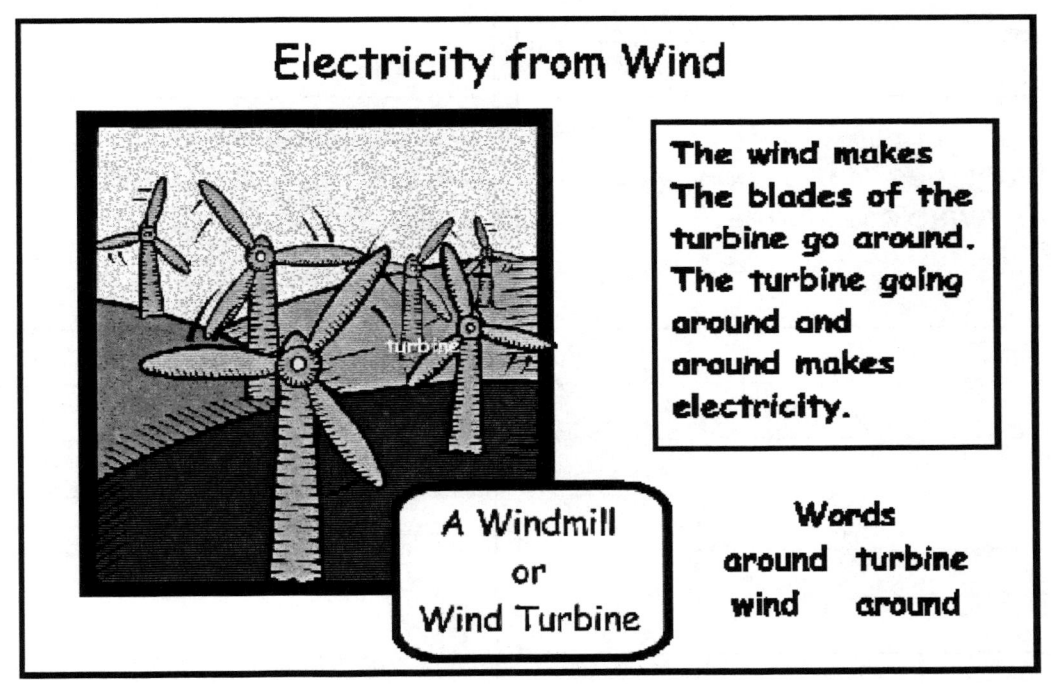

turbine

A Windmill or Wind Turbine

The wind makes The blades of the turbine go around. The turbine going around and around makes electricity.

Words
around   turbine
wind   around

BLM 2.7.3

Name _____

RENEWABLE SOURCES OF ENERGY

_ _ _ _ and _ _ _ _ _ _ _ _ _ _ _ are renewable sources of e _ _ _ _ _ .

Moving Water

Advantages of moving water as a renewable resource.
_____
_____
_____
_____
_____
_____

Disadvantages of moving water as a renewable resource.
_____
_____
_____
_____
_____
_____

Wind

Advantages of wind as a renewable resource.
_____
_____
_____
_____
_____
_____

Disadvantages of wind as a renewable resource.
_____
_____
_____
_____
_____
_____

BLM 2.7.4

Name _____

TEACHER RESOURCE
RENEWABLE SOURCES OF ENERGY

W i n d and m o v i n g w a t e r are renewable sources of e n e r g y.

Moving Water	Wind
Advantages of moving water as a renewable resource. Kind to the environment (non-polluting Once started water is free, Always available. Currently produces more electrical power than wind. **Disadvantages of moving water as a renewable resource.** Money needed to build the power plant. Need to have location with water, where hydroelectric plant can be built.	**Advantages of wind as a renewable resource.** Free once the wind turbine purchased. Non-polluting for wind, and soil. Quiet. **Disadvantages of wind as a renewable resource.** Start up cost - money to buy wind turbines. Weather must be suitable.

BLM 2.7.5

DESIGNING A WIND/ WATER POWERED DEVICE

Engineer: _____   Date: _____

Planning:

My device will be powered by _____ .

My blueprint of my device:

```
┌─────────────────────────────────────┐
│                                     │
│                                     │
│                                     │
│                                     │
│                                     │
│                                     │
│                                     │
│                                     │
└─────────────────────────────────────┘
```

BLM 2.8.1

Building:

Materials I will need:

_____
_____
_____
_____

Tools I will need:

_____
_____

Steps to build my device:

_____
_____
_____
_____
_____
_____
_____
_____

Explain any changes that were made:

_____
_____

Demonstrating:

1. How much load did your device carry?

   _____

   _____

   _____

2. How far did your device travel?

   _____

   _____

   _____

3. If you were to build your device again, what could you do to improve it?

   _____

   _____

   _____

   _____

RUBRIC FOR ASSESSING THE BUILDING PROCESS

Name: _____

Criteria	Level 1	Level 2	Level 3	Level 4
Designing — making a plan to solve the problem	- solution to the problem shows little understanding of the task - creates a sketch with no details	- solution to the problem shows some understanding of the task - creates a sketch which includes a few details	- solution to the problem shows a clear understanding of the task - creates a sketch which includes some details	- solution to the problem shows thorough understanding of the task - creates a sketch which includes many details
Building — carrying out the plan	- uses materials with limited assistance - uses few effective methods of fastening and joining	- uses materials with some assistance - uses some effective methods of fastening and joining	- uses material correctly with only occasional assistance - uses effective methods of fastening and joining	- uses materials correctly with little or no assistance - uses effective methods of fastening and joining
Testing — making sure things work	- requires assistance to test device after completion in order to see if it works as planned - changes only occur if suggested by others and if a great deal of assistance is given - records modifications made with little clarity	- requires some assistance to test device after completion in order to see if it works as planned - needs some encouragement to prompt changes and with some assistance - records modifications made with some clarity	- independently tests device after completion in order to see if it works as planned - realizes that changes are necessary and makes changes with only minimal assistance - clearly records modifications made	- independently tests device as it is being built and after completion in order to see if it works as planned - realizes that changes are necessary and makes changes independently - clearly and precisely records and justifies modifications made

BLM 2.8.4

RUBRIC FOR ASSESSING THE PRESENTATION TO THE CLASS   Name:

Criteria	Level 1	Level 2	Level 3	Level 4
Explanation - describe device, its construction and energy input	- uses limited scientific or technological words in explanation	- uses some scientific or technological words in explanation	- uses clear scientific or technological words in explanation	- uses many scientific or technological words in explanation
Oral Presentation	- presents with limited clarity	- presents with some clarity	- presents with clarity	- presents with clarity and precision

RUBRIC FOR ASSESSING THE PRESENTATION TO THE CLASS   Name:

Criteria	Level 1	Level 2	Level 3	Level 4
Explanation - describe device, its construction and energy input	- uses limited scientific or technological words in explanation	- uses some scientific or technological words in explanation	- uses clear scientific or technological words in explanation	- uses many scientific or technological words in explanation
Oral Presentation	- presents with limited clarity	- presents with some clarity	- presents with clarity	- presents with clarity and precision

BLM 2.8.5

RUBRIC FOR ASSESSING THE WIND/WATER POWERED DEVICE

Name: _____

Criteria	Level 1	Level 2	Level 3	Level 4
Construction	- device is somewhat complete, does not work, or does not use water or wind to propel it	- device is complete but does not work as planned	- device is complete and uses water or wind to propel it	- device is complete and uses water or wind effectively
Load	- does not support a load	- supports a load while stable	- supports a load over a distance	- supports a significant load over a distance
Speed	- has limited movement	- moves slowly	- moves quickly	- moves very quickly

BLM 2.8.6

SELF-ASSESSMENT FOR WIND/ WATER PROPELLED DEVICE TASK

Name: _____   Date:_____

Criteria	Yes	No
I drew a design of my device.		
I built a device powered by air or water.		
I used tools and materials properly.		
I tested my device and improved the design.		
My device carried a load of pennies over a distance.		
I completed a presentation of my device on time.		

The easiest part about doing this project was

_____

_____

_____

The hardest part about doing this project was

_____

_____

_____

Assessment Overview

Knowledge and Skills	Subtask 1: Anecdotal Record	Subtask 2: Rubric	Subtask 3: Checklist	Subtask 4: Checklist & Rubric	Subtask 5: Rubric	Subtask 6: Rubric	Subtask 7: Anecdotal Record	Subtask 8: Rubric Checklist
Understanding of basic concepts	X	X		X	X	X	X	X
Inquiry Skills			X	X				X
Design Skills								X
Communication Skills		X		X	X	X		X
Relating to the World		X	X	X	X	X		X

BLM 2.UW.1

ANECDOTAL RECORD SHEET

BLM 2.UW.2a

Anecdotal Record Sheet - Possible Teacher Comments

Cloe	Margarita	Pierre	Kong
Subtask 1 - participates frequently with related responses	**Subtask 1:** - unwilling to participate - responses inappropriate to topics	**Subtask 7:** - diagrams are complete and labelled accurately - appropriate responses given for cloze activity - contributes relevant ideas during group discussion - provides original, accurate responses about renewable sources of energy	**Subtask 7:** - diagrams are incomplete - lack detail - some inappropriate responses for cloze activity - off-task during group discussion - copies responses from chart with little understanding

BLM 2.UW.2b

I.N.S.I.T.E. Model of Inquiry

I -   Identify the problem

N -   Narrow the problem

S -   State the question and predict what will happen

I -   Investigate possible procedures and gather materials

T -   Test and trial

E -   Express your findings

I.N.S.I.T.E. Method

Throughout this unit students will be involved in inquiry based learning and investigations. This problem-solving model helps the students work through these investigations based on the principles of scientific inquiry called the I.N.S.I.T.E. method.

Identify the problem
Narrow the problem
State the hypothesis
Investigate and gather information
Test your hypothesis and record observations
Examine the results and write (communicate) conclusions

Identify the problem
The first step is for the students to identify the problem they will investigate or need to resolve.

Narrow the problem
The second step is to narrow the problem. At this stage the students will state the varied questions (what, when, where, how, why, etc.) related to the problem.

State the hypothesis
The third step is to state the hypothesis. In this statement the students will make a scientific guess as to what they believe will be a solution to the problem.

Investigate and gather information
The fourth step is for the students to conduct a scientific investigation related to the hypothesis. Students will need to conduct research and gather information related to the problem and the questions they generated in the second step. Once the students have enough background they will create a plan of investigation to test their hypothesis. The students will need to consider all the possible variables and constants in order to carry out a fair test. Plans should include a list of materials they will need.

Test the hypothesis and record observations
The fifth step is for the students to follow their plan and carry out a fair test to confirm the validity of their hypothesis. Students will record their observations as they test their hypothesis. Students should be given opportunity to use a variety of recording devices such as: charts, graphs, learning logs, or science journals.

Examine the results and write (communicate) conclusions
The sixth step is for the students to examine the results of their test and then write a conclusion (communicate a response) that outlines what they learned in the investigation and testing of their hypothesis. It is important that students examine their results and whether or not their hypothesis was valid before writing their conclusion. If their hypothesis was not valid the students may need to either develop a new hypothesis or create a new plan to test their hypothesis in order to gain different results. Students should examine what worked and why, what needs further research, and what needs further investigation. If their hypothesis was valid the students should state the solution to the problem in their conclusion and outline why it was a solution.

S.P.I.C.E. Model of Design

S = Situation
Observe the scene. Think about what has happened to create the problem.

P = Problems or Possibilities
Tell what the problem is and what the possible solutions to the problem might be.

I = Investigate/Ideas
Brainstorm as many solutions to the problem as possible. Think about materials, tools, people.

C = Choose/Construct
Choose the best idea. Plan your design and build it. Test your design to make sure it works.

E = Evaluate
Look back at the problem and think about how well you solved the problem.

* adapted from the SPICE model created by Geoff Day, University of Toronto, 1989

MY
SCIENCE AND TECHNOLOGY
JOURNAL

by _____

BLM 2.UW.5

Student Criteria for Science and Technology Journal

In my Science and Technology Journal, I will try to:

1. use science and technology words

2. give examples of things using words and pictures

3. tell all I know about what I did

4. give information to the reader

5. use capitals and periods in my sentences

SCIENCE AND TECHNOLOGY JOURNAL PAGE

BLM 2.UW.7

TITLE PAGE FOR THIS UNIT

ENERGY FROM WIND AND MOVING WATER

BLM 2.UW.8

SCIENCE AND TECHNOLOGY JOURNAL - ASSESSMENT RUBRIC

Name: _____

Skills	Level 1	Level 2	Level 3	Level 4
Understanding - understanding of relevant concepts (movement as an outcome of energy input, movement of air and water that produces energy, ways moving water is used) - explaining concepts	- demonstrates limited understanding of relevant concepts - demonstrates limited ability to make written and pictorial explantions that are complete, accurate, and detailed	- demonstrates some understanding of relevant concepts - demonstrates some ability to make written and pictorial explantions that are complete, accurate, and detailed	- demonstrates clear understanding of relevant concepts - written and pictorial explanations are complete, and accurate, and detailed	- demonstrates thorough understanding of relevant concepts - written and pictorial explanations are complete, accurate and extensively detailed

Communication
- independence
- writing of observations
- examples given
- vocabulary
  - energy
  - input
  - movement
  - renewable
  - hydroelectricity
  - control
	- writes ideas with assistance (needs much prompting)
	- provides a few examples through words and/or pictures
	- rarely uses scientific vocabulary
		- writes ideas with limited assistance (needs some prompting)
		- provides some examples using words and/or pictures
		- sometimes uses scientific vocabulary
			- independently writes ideas (no prompting needed)
			- provides several examples using words and pictures
			- generally uses scientific vocabulary
				- independently and confidential writes ideas
				- provides many, detailed examples using words and pictures
				- consistenly uses scientific vocabulary

Relating to the World -windmills and water wheels -activities affected by moving water and wind -gravity	- shows limited understanding of how wind and movingwater are used in familiar contexts and in the world	- shows some understanding of how wind and moving water are used in familiar contexts and in the world	- shows clear understanding of how wind and moving water are used in familiar contexts and in the world	- shows thorough understanding of how windand moving water are used in familiar contexts and in the world

BLM 2.UW.9

Energy from Wind and Moving Water
Energy and Control An Integrated Unit for Grade 2

Expectation List
Page 1

Selected | Assessed

Science and Technology---Energy and Control

☐ 2s49	• demonstrate an understanding of the movement of air and of water as sources of energy;	6
☐ 2s50	• design and construct devices that are propelled by moving air or moving water;	6
☐ 2s51	• identify wind and moving water as renewable sources of energy and determine the advantages and disadvantages of using them.	4
☐ 2s52	– identify movement as an outcome of energy input (e.g., fuel enables cars, trucks, and buses to move; electricity enables the fan in the kitchen to move; food enables humans to move);	1
☐ 2s53	– recognize that it is the movement of air and water that produces energy and that air and water are not by themselves sources of energy;	3
☐ 2s54	– identify various ways in which moving water is used as a form of energy (e.g., hydroelectricity, tidal energy).	1
☐ 2s55	– design and construct a device propelled by air (e.g., a kite, a pinwheel, a balloon rocket);	1
☐ 2s56	– design and construct a system that controls the flow of water and/or air using a variety of mechanisms (e.g., a musical instrument, a fountain, valves, a dam);	1
☐ 2s57	– ask questions about and identify needs and problems related to the use of wind and moving water as energy sources, and explore possible answers and solutions (e.g., describe how moving water is used to produce electricity; describe how windmills were used to grind grain into flour);	4
☐ 2s58	– plan investigations to answer some of these questions or solve some of these problems, and describe the steps involved;	1
☐ 2s59	– use appropriate vocabulary in describing their investigations, explorations, and observations (e.g., use terms such as renewable and movement when describing energy);	2
☐ 2s60	– record relevant observations, findings, and measurements, using written language, pictures, and charts (e.g., draw a diagram of their device; prepare a chart to present data on the distance travelled by their device over time);	2
☐ 2s61	– communicate the procedures and results of investigations and explorations for specific purposes, using drawings, demonstrations, and oral and written descriptions (e.g., prepare a showcase of different devices that are propelled by wind energy; explain the effect of wind direction and speed on the displacement of wind-propelled devices).	2
☐ 2s62	– identify devices that use moving air and moving water as energy sources (e.g., windmills, water wheels), and describe what happens to these devices when the air or water is still;	2
☐ 2s63	– list activities that are affected by moving water and wind (e.g., fishing, sailing, flying a plane);	2
☐ 2s64	– recognize that moving air and moving water can be sources of energy for electrical power;	1
☐ 2s65	– describe how gravity and the shape of different structures affect the behaviour and use of moving water (e.g., water in waterfalls, taps, fountains).	1

Energy from Wind and Moving Water
Energy and Control An Integrated Unit for Grade 2

Expectation Summary
Selected | Assessed

English Language
2e1	2e2	2e3	2e4	2e5	2e6	2e7	2e8	2e9	2e10
2e11	2e12	2e13	2e14	2e15	2e16	2e17	2e18	2e19	2e20
2e21	2e22	2e23	2e24	2e25	2e26	2e27	2e28	2e29	2e30
2e31	2e32	2e33	2e34	2e35	2e36	2e37	2e38	2e39	2e40
2e41	2e42	2e43	2e44	2e45	2e46	2e47	2e48	2e49	2e50
2e51	2e52	2e53	2e54	2e55	2e56	2e57	2e58	2e59	2e60
2e61	2e62	2e63	2e64	2e65					

Mathematics
2m1	2m2	2m3	2m4	2m5	2m6	2m7	2m8	2m9	2m10
2m11	2m12	2m13	2m14	2m15	2m16	2m17	2m18	2m19	2m20
2m21	2m22	2m23	2m24	2m25	2m26	2m27	2m28	2m29	2m30
2m31	2m32	2m33	2m34	2m35	2m36	2m37	2m38	2m39	2m40
2m41	2m42	2m43	2m44	2m45	2m46	2m47	2m48	2m49	2m50
2m51	2m52	2m53	2m54	2m55	2m56	2m57	2m58	2m59	2m60
2m61	2m62	2m63	2m64	2m65	2m66	2m67	2m68	2m69	2m72
2m73	2m74	2m75	2m70	2m71	2m76	2m77	2m78	2m79	2m80
2m81	2m82	2m83	2m84	2m85	2m86	2m87	2m88	2m89	2m90
2m91	2m92	2m93	2m94	2m95	2m96	2m97	2m98	2m99	2m100
2m101	2m102	2m103	2m104	2m105	2m106	2m107	2m108	2m109	2m110
2m111	2m112								

Science and Technology
2s1	2s2	2s3	2s4	2s5	2s6	2s7	2s8	2s9	2s10
2s11	2s12	2s13	2s14	2s15	2s16	2s17	2s18	2s19	2s20
2s21	2s22	2s23	2s24	2s25	2s26	2s27	2s28	2s29	2s30
2s31	2s32	2s33	2s34	2s35	2s36	2s37	2s38	2s39	2s40
2s41	2s42	2s43	2s44	2s45	2s46	2s47	2s48	2s49 6	2s50 6
2s51 4	2s52 1	2s53 3	2s54 1	2s55 1	2s56 1	2s57 4	2s58 1	2s59 2	2s60 2
2s61 2	2s62 2	2s63 2	2s64 1	2s65 1	2s66	2s67	2s68	2s69	2s70
2s71	2s72	2s73	2s74	2s75	2s76	2s77	2s78	2s79	2s80
2s81	2s82	2s83	2s84	2s85	2s86	2s87	2s88	2s89	2s90
2s91	2s92	2s93	2s94	2s95	2s96	2s97	2s98	2s99	2s100
2s101	2s102	2s103	2s104	2s105	2s106	2s107	2s108	2s109	2s110

Social Studies
2z1	2z2	2z3	2z4	2z5	2z6	2z7	2z8	2z9	2z10
2z11	2z12	2z13	2z14	2z15	2z16	2z17	2z18	2z19	2z20
2z21	2z22	2z23	2z24	2z25	2z26	2z27	2z28	2z29	2z30
2z31	2z32	2z33	2z34	2z35	2z36	2z37	2z38	2z39	2z40
2z41	2z42	2z43	2z44	2z45	2z46	2z47	2z48		

Health & Physical Education
2p1	2p2	2p3	2p4	2p5	2p6	2p7	2p8	2p9	2p10
2p11	2p12	2p13	2p14	2p15	2p16	2p17	2p18	2p19	2p20
2p21	2p22	2p23	2p24	2p25	2p26	2p27	2p28	2p29	2p30
2p31	2p32	2p33	2p34	2p35	2p36	2p37	2p38	2p39	2p40
2p41									

The Arts
2a1	2a2	2a3	2a4	2a5	2a6	2a7	2a8	2a9	2a10
2a11	2a12	2a13	2a14	2a15	2a16	2a17	2a18	2a19	2a20
2a21	2a22	2a23	2a24	2a25	2a26	2a27	2a28	2a29	2a30
2a31	2a32	2a33	2a34	2a35	2a36	2a37	2a38	2a39	2a40
2a41	2a42	2a43	2a44	2a45	2a46	2a47	2a48	2a49	2a50
2a51	2a52	2a53	2a54	2a55	2a56	2a57	2a58	2a59	2a60
2a61	2a62	2a63	2a64	2a65	2a66	2a67			

Energy from Wind and Moving Water
Energy and Control An Integrated Unit for Grade 2

Unit Analysis
Page 1

Analysis Of Unit Components

- 8 Subtasks
- 40 Expectations
- 149 Resources
- 82 Strategies & Groupings

-- Unique Expectations --
- 17 Science And Tech Expectations

Resource Types

- 0 Rubrics
- 49 Blackline Masters
- 0 Licensed Software
- 9 Print Resources
- 2 Media Resources
- 0 Websites
- 65 Material Resources
- 24 Equipment / Manipulatives
- 0 Sample Graphics
- 0 Other Resources
- 0 Parent / Community
- 0 Companion Bookmarks

Groupings

- 8 Students Working As A Whole Class
- 1 Students Working In Pairs
- 5 Students Working In Small Groups
- 8 Students Working Individually

Teaching / Learning Strategies

- 1 Brainstorming
- 1 Collaborative/cooperative Learning
- 3 Demonstration
- 1 Direct Teaching
- 7 Discussion
- 1 Experimenting
- 1 Inquiry
- 6 Learning Log/ Journal
- 4 Model Making
- 3 Oral Explanation
- 1 Problem Posing
- 1 Rehearsal / Repetition / Practice
- 1 Sketching To Learn

Assessment Recording Devices

- 2 Anecdotal Record
- 3 Checklist
- 5 Rubric

Assessment Strategies

- 1 Classroom Presentation
- 2 Exhibition/demonstration
- 4 Learning Log
- 4 Observation
- 1 Performance Task
- 3 Questions And Answers (oral)
- 2 Response Journal
- 1 Select Response
- 1 Self Assessment

Written using the **Ontario Curriculum Unit Planner** 2.51 PLNR_01 March, 2001* Open Printed on Sep 09, 2001 at 5:09:43 PM Page H-1